TITLE:

THE PSYCHOLOGY OF SEX:

Exploring The Intricate Processes Underlying Sexual Arousal, Desire, Behavior, And Relationships .

Rosa

All rights reserved. No part of this publication may be reproduced, distributed or transmitted in any form or by any means, including photocopying, recording or other electronic or mechanical methods, without the prior written permission of the publisher, except in the case of brief quotations embodied in critical reviews and certain other non-commercial uses permitted by copyright law © (Rosalie L. Crawford), (2024).

TABLE OF CONTENTS

CHAPTER ONE: 6
Introduction to Sexual Psychology: 7
The Meaning of Sexual Psychology: 9
Historical Views on the Study of Human Sexuality: 12
The Value of Knowing About Sexual Psychology: 15
Important Terms and Ideas in Sexual Psychology: 18
CHAPTER TWO 21
The Basic Biochemical Basis of Sexuality: 22
Human Sexual Response's Anatomy and Physiology: 25
HORMONAL INFLUENCES ON SEXUAL BEHAVIOR: 28
Evolutionary Views of Human Sexuality: 31
The influence of genetics on sexual orientation: 34
CHAPTER THREE 37
Sexual Development And Psychology: 38
Development of Sexuality Throughout Life 42
The Influence of Culture and Family on Sexual Beliefs: 45
Forming a Sexual Identity: 48
Psychological Difficulties Associated with Sexual Development: 50
CHAPTER FOUR 54
Sexual Desire and Arousal: 55
Understanding Sexual Arousal Patterns: 58
The psychological and emotional dimensions of sexual attraction: 62
Individual Variations in Sexual Desire: 65
CHAPTER FIVE 68
Relationships, Love, and Intimacy: 69
The Psychology of Love: 72
Relationship dynamics and attachment theory: 76
Intimacy Development in Romantic Relationship: 79
Sexual Satisfaction and Quality Relationship: 82
CHAPTER SIX 87
Sexual Expression and Behavior: 88
Variations in Sexual Behavior: 92
Sexual Fantasies and Preoccupations: 95
Social and Cultural Influences on Sexual Expression: 98
Handling Problems with Sexual Functions: 101

CHAPTER SEVEN 105

Gender and Sexuality: 106

Gender Identity and Sexual Orientation: 110

Transgender and Non-Binary Experiences: 114

The intersections of mental health, sexuality, and gender: 117

Problems and Shame Experiencing LGBTQ+ People: 120

CHAPTER EIGHT: 123

Sexuality and Mental Health: 124

Psychological Disorders Affecting Sexual Functioning: 127

.Trauma and Sexual Wellness: 129

Resilience Techniques for Sexual and Mental Health Issues: 133

The Value of Counseling and Therapy for Handling Sexual Issues: 136

CHAPTER NINE 139

Sexuality, media, and technology: 140

The impact of media on attitudes and behaviors related to sexuality: 143

Online and Digital Trends in Sexuality: 146

Ethical Issues with How Sexuality Is Represented in the Media: 151

Positive and Negative effects of Technology on Sexual Health: 154

CHAPTER TEN 159

Education and Advocacy on Sexuality: 160

Full Sexual Education's Significance: 165

Advocacy for Sexual Health and Rights: 169

Addressing Sexual Violence and Consent: 172

Encouraging Healthy Practices in Sexuality: 177

CHAPTER ELEVEN 1280

Global and Cultural Views on Sexuality: 181

Sexual Norms and Practices Vary by Culture: 185

Global Difficulties Sexual Health: 188

Research on Sexuality Across Cultures: 192

Techniques for Encouraging Sexual Health Equity: 197

CHAPTER TWELVE 200

Future Tendencies in Sexual Psychology: 201

Developing Fields of Study in Sexual Psychology: 206

Topics of Interest for Future Sexual Psychology Research: 210

The Promotion of Diversity and Inclusivity in Sexual Psychology: 213

Advancing Sexual Research: Ethical Considerations: 217

CHAPTER THIRTEEN 219

In Conclusion: 221

The Significance of Continued Research and Education: 224

Empowering People for Healthy and Fulfilling Sexual Lives: 226

CHAPTER ONE:

Introduction to Sexual Psychology:

The study of the complex interactions between psychological processes and human sexuality is the focus of the intriguing field of sexual psychology. Exploring the intricate processes underlying sexual arousal, desire, behavior, and relationships, it illuminates basic facets of human nature that influence our close encounters.

In the past, there has been debate and interest in the study of human sexuality. From Freud's psychoanalytic theories to contemporary neurobiological and cognitive psychology studies, sexual psychology has undergone substantial development and provided valuable insights into our perceptions of intimacy, pleasure, and identity.

The fundamental idea of sexual psychology is that sexuality is a complex process that is shaped by social, cultural, psychological, and biological elements. It covers a wide range of subjects, such as the influence of media and technology on sexual attitudes and behaviors, sexual development, gender identity, sexual orientation, interpersonal relationships, and sexual health.

Understanding the intricacies of sexual arousal and desire is one of the main goals of sexual psychology. Researchers look at the ways that hormone swings and brain circuits, among other physiological processes, interact with emotional and cognitive elements to influence our sexual experiences. Understanding these systems not only contributes to our knowledge of human sexuality but also informs therapeutic interventions for persons with sexual problems or dysfunctions.

Furthermore, sexual psychology studies how social and cultural factors shape our attitudes, behaviors, and beliefs about sexuality. Our sexual identities and manifestations are shaped in part by religious convictions, cultural standards, societal expectations, and media representations. The point at which psychology and culture converge is that studying sexuality requires taking into account a variety of viewpoints and experiences.

This book takes us on a fascinating tour through the field of sexual psychology, examining its many facets and consequences for both society understanding and personal well-being. We seek to present a thorough overview that highlights the diversity and complexity of human sexuality by exploring issues like sexual development, desire, relationships, gender identity, mental health, and cultural perspectives.

We encourage readers to interact critically and compassionately with the range of experiences and difficulties associated with sexuality by means of an interdisciplinary approach that combines psychological theories, research findings, clinical insights, and first-hand accounts. In the end, we want to promote a better comprehension of the psychology of sex and how it affects relationships, societies, and individual lives.

The Meaning of Sexual Psychology:

Understanding and researching human sexuality from a psychological standpoint is the main goal of sexual psychology, a subfield of psychology. It covers a broad spectrum of subjects pertaining to sexual experiences, acts, feelings, and thoughts. This area of study examines the intricate interactions of biological, psychological, social, cultural, and environmental elements that influence people's sexual identities and expressions.

The fundamental goal of sexual psychology is to understand the complexities of intimacy, arousal, attraction, and sexual desire. It looks at how people view, feel, and express their sexuality in addition to the psychological mechanisms that underpin the formation and operation of the sex.

Studying sexual growth over the course of a person's lifetime is a crucial component of sexual psychology. Examining how people's sexual views, beliefs, and practices change as they grow from childhood to adolescence to adulthood and beyond is part of this. In order to promote healthy sexual attitudes and behaviors and address concerns linked to sexual identity formation, sexual health, and sexual well-being, it is imperative to have a thorough understanding of the psychological elements that influence sexual development.

Along with examining differences in sexual orientation, gender identity, sexual preferences, and sexual behaviors, sexual psychology also examines the diversity of human sexual experiences. Recognizing and appreciating the vast range of sexual variation, it seeks to offer a thorough grasp of the psychological elements of sexuality in many demographics.

Moreover, the psychological aspects of intimate relationships and sexual interactions are explored by sexual psychology. It looks at things like how to resolve conflicts and communicate, trust, be intimate, and feel satisfied in romantic relationships and sexual interactions. Sexual psychology helps individuals and couples overcome obstacles connected to sexual intimacy and connection by researching these areas. It also provides insights into the intricacies of human relationships.

Sexual health and well-being constitute a significant subfield of sexual psychology. Sexual dysfunction, sexual disorders, sexual trauma, sexual violence, contraception, STIs, and reproductive health are among the concerns that need to be addressed. Sexual psychology plays an important role in improving sexual health education, preventive, and intervention techniques by fusing psychological concepts with medical and public health approaches.

In summary, the study of sexual psychology is dynamic and interdisciplinary, bridging the disciplines of medicine, ethics, biology, sociology, anthropology, and psychology. By addressing the intricate psychological aspects of human sexual experiences, it seeks to increase consciousness, expand knowledge, and cultivate healthy attitudes toward sexuality.

Historical Views on the Study of Human Sexuality:

With nations and cultures struggling to comprehend and interpret human sexual experiences, the study of sexuality has a long and varied history. The evolution of concepts and attitudes toward sexuality has been influenced by a wide range of philosophical, religious, scientific, and cultural factors throughout history.

Early Philosophical Thought and Ancient Civilizations: - Sex was frequently entwined with religious activities and beliefs in ancient societies including Mesopotamia, Egypt, Greece, and Rome. There were deities in many ancient societies who were linked to sexuality, love, and fertility, and sexuality-related rituals were widespread.
- The nature of desire, love, and pleasure was studied by early philosophers like Plato and Aristotle. Aristotle's writings touch on the psychological components of sexual desire, whereas Plato's "Symposium" addresses several sorts of love, including erotic love.

Medieval and Renaissance Perspectives: - Christian teachings, which frequently saw sexuality in the framework of sin and virtue, had a significant influence on Western society during the medieval era. The Church's teachings on marriage, celibacy, and sexual morality influenced society perceptions of sexuality. More complex conversations about love, beauty, and desire resulted from the Renaissance's revival of interest in humanism and the arts. Human bodies and sensual themes were portrayed in the works of writers and artists like Michelangelo and Leonardo da Vinci.

Scientific Research and Enlightenment: - A move toward reason and science during the Enlightenment led academics to investigate sexuality from both an empirical and philosophical standpoint. Individual rights and freedoms were championed by thinkers such as John Locke and Denis Diderot, who questioned conventional beliefs on sexuality. Scientific studies of human sexuality were made possible by the advancements in anatomy and medicine during the Enlightenment.

Havelock Ellis and Richard von Krafft-Ebing were among the first sexologists to start scientifically examining sexual identities and behaviors.

Freudian psychoanalysis and the Victorian era: - Strict social conventions and taboos around sexuality, especially in Western societies, defined the Victorian era in the 19th century. Sexuality-related conversations were frequently suppressed or limited to moral and medical domains. With the development of his psychoanalytic theories in the late 19th and early 20th century, Sigmund Freud transformed the field of sexuality studies. By examining the unconscious mind, early experiences, and suppressed impulses, Freud illuminated the psychological intricacies of sexual behavior and growth.

20th-Century and Contemporary Views: - Significant developments in the study of sexuality occurred in the 20th century, including the emergence of sexology as a separate discipline of study. Researchers who made significant contributions to the field of sexual behavior, orientation, and dysfunction included Evelyn Hooker, Alfred Kinsey, and Masters and Johnson. Advocating for women's rights, LGBTQ+ visibility, sexual liberation, and reproductive liberties, the sexual revolution of the 1960s and 1970s upended conventional sexual norms and attitudes.
"- Modern methods for studying sexuality draw on multidisciplinary insights from fields such as gender studies, public health, biology, sociology, psychology, and anthropology. Modern conversations on sexuality revolve around issues including sexual orientation, gender identity, sexual health, consent, and diversity.

Overall, historical viewpoints on the study of sexuality show how cultural, social, political, and scientific variables have produced a dynamic and changing discourse. The study of human sexuality has always been a complex and vital part of comprehending human nature and society, from prehistoric ceremonies to contemporary research.

The Value of Knowing About Sexual Psychology:

For many reasons, knowing the psychology of sex is important for individuals, groups, and societies as a whole. The significance of this comprehension is emphasized by the following numerous salient points:

Personal Development, Self-Acceptance, and General Well-Being: Recognizing one's own sexuality and sexual identity is crucial for human development. It promotes emotional fulfillment and self-confidence by assisting people in navigating their relationships, limits, and desires in a healthy and gratifying way.

2. Healthy Relationships: Communication, trust, intimacy, and conflict resolution are all aspects of intimate relationship dynamics that are illuminated by sexual psychology. People may create happier, better relationships based on empathy, consent, and respect by learning about the psychological components of sex and relationships.

3. Sexual Health: In order to promote sexual health and avoid sexual difficulties and disorders, it is essential to have an understanding of sexual psychology. It supports people in making knowledgeable decisions regarding STI prevention, sexual consent, contraception, and getting the right medical attention when they have sexual health issues.

4. Reducing Shame and Stigma: By recognizing the range of sexual identities, preferences, and orientations, we may promote inclusivity and lessen the shame and stigma attached to non-normative sexual conduct. This encourages tolerance, acceptance, and support for people with varying sexual orientations.

5. Preventing Sexual Violence: Fostering a Consent Culture and Stopped Sexual Violence are Made Possible by Understanding Sexual Psychology. It enables people to identify and confront damaging attitudes, convictions, and actions that support sexual coercion, harassment, and assault.

6. Gender Equality: Works toward gender equality and empowerment are aided by the understanding of the relationship between gender, power relations, and sexuality provided by sexual psychology. It promotes equal connections and opportunities for people of all genders by challenging conventional gender norms and stereotypes.

7. Parenting and Education: In order to successfully teach children and adolescents about sexuality, parents, teachers, and other caregivers must have a thorough understanding of sexual psychology. In an age-appropriate and encouraging way, it facilitates conversations about consent, healthy relationships, limits, and sexual health.

8. Mental Health and Well-Being: The psychological components of sexual dysfunctions, disorders, trauma, and issues with mental health that are connected to sexuality are treated by sexual psychology. In order to treat these problems and advance general mental health, it highlights the significance of therapy, counseling, and support services.

9. Cultural and Social Change: Sexual psychology insights support social change movements and cultural transformations that fight discrimination, support LGBTQ+ rights, and advance sexual health equity. It promotes candid discussion, instruction, and activism in support of positive social norms and perspectives around sexuality.

10. Research and Innovation: Advances in therapies, interventions, and policies pertaining to sexual health and well-being are fueled by ongoing research in sexual psychology. It provides guidance for evidence-based policies, procedures, and initiatives that try to enhance the lives of both people and communities.

Ultimately, a society that values sexual health, rights, and dignity for all people must be knowledgeable, empathetic, and inclusive, and this requires an understanding of the psychology of sex. In navigating the complexity of human sexuality, it promotes a culture of tolerance, acceptance, and empowerment.

Important Terms and Ideas in Sexual Psychology:

The intricate interaction of biological, psychological, social, and cultural elements that shape a person's ideas, feelings, behaviors, and experiences related to sex is known as sexuality.

2. Sexual Orientation: A persistent pattern of romantic, affective, and sexual attraction to people who belong to a specific gender or genders. The following are common orientations: asexual, bisexual, gay, and heterosexual.

3. Gender Identity: The internal feeling of gender that a person has, which might or might not match the sex they were given at birth. Gender identities encompass a range of identities, such as non-binary, transgender, genderqueer, and male and female.

4. Sexual Identity: How people interpret and categorize their own sexual preferences and orientation, which can change over the course of a lifetime in terms of complexity and fluidity.

5. Sexual Desire: The motivational condition that pushes people to look for opportunities for sexual contact and experiences. It can be impacted by biological, psychological, and social variables and range in intensity.

6. Sexual Arousal: A physiological and psychological reaction to sexual stimuli that results in heightened sensitivity, increased blood flow to the genitalia, and subjective emotions of excitement.

7. Sexual Response Cycle: This is the series of mental and physical phases that people usually go through when they engage in sexual activity. These phases include resolve, arousal, desire, plateau, and climax.

8. Intimacy: The state of emotional intimacy, trust, and connection between people; frequently accompanied by sentiments of warmth, love, and understanding. Physical contact, emotional support, and honest conversation are all ways to demonstrate intimacy.

9. Consent: Mutual consent to sexual activity that is given voluntarily and is marked by open communication, respect for personal space, and the lack of coercion or manipulation. Consent must be continuous and can be reversed at any time.

10. Sexual health: A state of well-being regarding one's sexuality that includes physical, emotional, mental, and social aspects. It includes things like having safe and enjoyable sex, maintaining good reproductive health, avoiding STIs, and having access to healthcare and sexual education.

11. Sexual dysfunction is the term used to describe ongoing issues or challenges pertaining to arousal, orgasm, desire, or pain that prevent a person from having fulfilling sexual experiences. Vaginismus, low libido, early ejaculation, and erectile dysfunction are examples of common sexual dysfunctions.

12. Sexual trauma: psychological anguish or injury brought on by encounters with sexual assault, abuse, harassment, or violence. Relationships, mental health, and sexual well-being are all susceptible to the long-term repercussions of sexual trauma.

13. Gender dysphoria: The state of distress or unease felt by people whose gender identity does not correspond with the sex they were given at birth. Emotional

distress, social challenges, and physical characteristic dissatisfaction are some of the manifestations of gender dysphoria.

Lesbian, gay, bisexual, transgender, queer, questioning, and other individuals who identify as LGBTQ+ or who have non-normative gender identities or sexual orientations are considered sexual minorities. Sexual minorities could experience discrimination, stigma, and obstacles to getting medical care and social acceptance.

15. Sexual Education: This all-inclusive, developmentally appropriate course covers topics such as consent, STI prevention, sexual health, partnerships, contraception, and reproductive rights. The goals of sexual education are to encourage responsible decision-making, wholesome lifestyle choices, and respectful views on sexuality.

In the context of sexual psychology, these fundamental ideas and terms are essential to comprehending the intricacies of human sexuality, psychological functions, and interpersonal interactions. They offer a framework for talking about and looking into the various aspects, difficulties, and experiences that people have with sexuality in both themselves and their communities.

CHAPTER TWO

The Basic Biochemical Basis of Sexuality:

Anatomy, physiology, hormones, genetics, and other biological systems are closely linked to sexuality. Comprehending the biological bases of sexuality offers valuable understanding of the processes that underpin arousal, behavior, and sexual growth. Key elements of the biological underpinnings of sexuality are as follows:

1. The Physiology and Anatomy of Sexual Organs
Male anatomy: The vas deferens, seminal vesicles, prostate gland, penis, testes, epididymis, and urethra comprise the male reproductive system. The two most important physiological processes during sexual engagement are erection and ejaculation.
The vagina, uterus, ovaries, fallopian tubes, clitoris, labia, and breasts make up the female reproductive system, according to female anatomy. The three main processes of female reproductive physiology are ovulation, pregnancy, and menstruation.

2. Sexual Response Cycle: The four stages of the sexual response cycle—excitation, plateau, orgasm, and resolution—are delineated by Masters and Johnson's model. These phases are characterized by physiological alterations such heightened blood flow to the sexual organs, contractions of the muscles, and release of hormones.
With an emphasis on psychological elements like desire, arousal, and satisfaction, Kaplan's triphasic model gives the sexual response cycle a subjective element.

3. Hormonal Influences: - Testosterone: Mostly produced in the ovaries of females and the testes of males, testosterone is essential for libido, sexual arousal, and secondary sexual traits (e.g., facial hair, muscle mass).
- Estrogen and progesterone: mostly generated in the ovaries, these hormones affect ovulation, menstrual cycles, and female sexual receptivity.

- Oxytocin and Vasopressin: Also referred to as "bonding hormones," these two chemicals have a role in social bonding, attachment, and pair bonding within intimate partnerships.

4. Sexual Differentiation and Development: - Sex hormones, environmental circumstances, and genetic factors (XX for females, XY for males) influence sexual differentiation during fetal development. The formation of basic and secondary sexual traits, together with the sexual differentiation of the brain, are factors that influence an individual's sexual identity and orientation.

5. Reproductive Health and Fertility: - Sexual health includes reproductive health, which includes menstruation, STIs, contraception, fertility, and reproductive technology (such as in vitro fertilization).
- Reproductive health and sexual performance can be impacted by a number of factors, including age, hormonal balance, lifestyle choices, and illnesses.

6. Neurobiology of Pleasure and Reward: - Reward systems in the brain, such as those found in the prefrontal cortex and nucleus accumbens, are involved in sexual pleasure, motivation, and behavior reinforcement.
- Feelings of pleasure, arousal, and emotional bonding during sexual experiences are facilitated by neurotransmitters including dopamine, serotonin, and endorphins.

Seventh, Genetics and Sexual Orientation: Research indicates that sexual orientation is influenced by genetics, however sexual orientation is not solely determined by genetics. Complex interactions between genetic, hormonal, and environmental factors shape sexual identity and desire.

Comprehending the biological underpinnings of sexuality is crucial in tackling matters pertaining to sexual health, advocating for well-informed choices, and propelling investigations and remedies in the fields of sexual psychology and medicine. It emphasizes how social, psychological, and biological variables interact intricately to shape human sexuality.

Human Sexual Response's Anatomy and Physiology:

Biological mechanisms that are involved in sexual arousal, stimulation, and orgasm are intricately intertwined in the anatomy and physiology of the human sexual response. It is vital to appreciate these systems in order to understand the physical components of sexual functioning and activity. An outline of the main elements that make up the anatomy and physiology of the human sexual response is provided below:

1. Sexual Structures and Organs:
- Anatomy of Men:
- Penis: Made up of erectile tissue, the corpus cavernosum and corpus spongiosum comprise the penis. Increased blood flow during excitement causes an erection, which facilitates penetration during sexual activity.
- Testes: The testes generate sperm and testosterone. For males to develop secondary sexual traits, sexual arousal, and libido, testosterone is essential.
- Prostate Gland: Fluids secreted by the prostate gland influence ejaculation and the composition of semen.
- Female Anatomy:
- Clitoris: At the summit of the vulva is the extremely sensitive clitoris organ. It is essential to female arousal and sexual satisfaction because it contains erectile tissue.
- Vagina: The vagina is a muscular channel that joins the cervix and external genitalia. It makes penetration easier during sex and acts as a conduit for menstruation and delivery.
- Ovaries: The ovaries are the source of progesterone, estrogen, and ova. These hormones control a woman's ovulation, fertility, and menstrual cycle.

2. The Cycle of Sexual Response:
- Excitement Phase: When a person is sexually aroused, their body goes through several changes. These include enhanced blood flow to their sexual organs, female vaginal lubrication, male erection, and greater sensory perception.

- Plateau Phase: Sex excitement increases, accompanied by increased muscle tension, heart rate, blood pressure, and erectile tissue engorgement.
- Orgasmic Phase: Those who are stimulated further achieve an orgasm, which is marked by strong pleasure, a release of sexual tension, and rhythmic muscle contractions. The central nervous system, pelvic muscles, and genital organs are all involved in orgasm.
- Resolution Phase: The body progressively returns to its pre-arousal state following an orgasm, characterized by decreased blood flow, musculoskeletal relaxation, and a feeling of contentment or refractory period (in males).

3. Hormonal Influences: - Testosterone: This hormone is essential for both male and female desire, sexual stimulation, and the preservation of sexual function. Male testes and female ovaries/adrenal glands are the main places where it is generated.
- Estrogen and Progesterone: These are female sex hormones that help to lubricate the vagina, control menstrual cycles, and increase desire and receptivity.
- Oxytocin: Often called the "love hormone," oxytocin is released when giving birth, bonding, and sexual activity. It fosters closeness, trust, and attachment feelings.

Neurological Processes: - Brain Regions: The limbic system, prefrontal cortex, amygdala, and hypothalamus are among the brain regions involved in sexual arousal and response. These brain regions control motivation, emotions, pleasure, and sensory processing during intercourse.
- Neurotransmitters: The brain's reward system is mediated by dopamine, serotonin, and endorphins, which are known to contribute to sensations of pleasure, desire, and emotional bonding during sexual activity.

5. Reproductive Function: - Fertility: When sperm cells from the male reproductive system come into contact with eggs (ova) released from the ovaries during ovulation, sexual activity can result in fertilization. Usually, fertilization takes place in the fallopian tubes, and if it is successful, pregnancy results.
- Ejaculation and Orgasm: Ejaculation in males is the process of ejecting semen from the penis during an orgasm, which facilitates the movement of sperm in

preparation for possible fertilization. Orgasm in females is linked to sexual pleasure and bonding but is not directly related to reproductive function.

Comprehending the human sexual response's anatomy and physiology is essential for managing sexual health issues, enhancing sexual encounters, and encouraging well-informed choices regarding intimacy and sexual engagement. It draws attention to the complex biological mechanisms that underpin sexual desire, behavior, and reproductive processes in people.

HORMONAL INFLUENCES ON SEXUAL BEHAVIOR:

Hormonal factors are known to have a notable impact on sexual behavior, as they regulate sexual function and behavior in both males and females. These hormones, which are produced by different endocrine system glands, aid in the development of sexual traits, libido (sexual desire), arousal, and reproductive functions. The following are the main hormones that affect sexual behavior:

1. The hormone testosterone

Testosterone's involvement in male sexual development is important to the growth of the penis, the testes, and secondary sexual traits including facial hair, muscle bulk, and deepening of voice. Testosterone is predominantly produced in the testes. Additionally, it is essential for sexual arousal, desire, and maintaining erectile function.

- Role in Females: Testosterone contributes to female sexual function, albeit in lesser amounts than in males. It enhances sexual desire, libido, and the sensitivity of erogenous zones like the clitoris. In females, the adrenal glands and ovaries create testosterone.

2. Estriol:

- Function in Females: The development of female sexual traits, including as the formation of breasts, control over the menstrual cycle, and preservation of vaginal health, depend on estrogen, which is mostly produced in the ovaries. Estrogen might affect sexual receptivity and desire since it peaks during ovulation and varies throughout the menstrual cycle.

- Function in Males: Although it is found in lesser quantities in men, estrogen is nevertheless important for male sexual function. It supports cardiovascular health, libido management, and bone density maintenance.

3. The hormone progesterone

- Function in Females: The ovaries also generate progesterone, which is involved in the menstrual cycle and pregnancy. It assists in regulating ovulation, gets the uterus ready for the implantation of a fertilized egg, and keeps the pregnancy going. During various stages of the menstrual cycle, progesterone levels can affect mood and libido.

The creation of sperm and the control of testosterone levels are two functions of progesterone, which is also generated in modest amounts by males.

4. Oxytocin:

- The pituitary gland releases oxytocin, which is sometimes referred to as the "love hormone" or "bonding hormone." It is produced in the hypothalamus. Intimacy, including sexual intimacy, emotional attachment, and social bonding are all impacted by it. It is possible for oxytocin levels to rise during pregnancy, bonding, and intimate times.

5. Estradiol:

The main function of prolactin is in the lactation process, which is the production of milk by women after giving birth. It also affects libido, refractory periods (the interval following an orgasm during which additional arousal is blocked), and sexual satisfaction, which all have an impact on sexual behavior. After an orgasm, prolactin levels could rise.

6. Hormones of Stress and Cortisol:

Cortisol and other stress hormones have an effect on sexual function and behavior. Prolonged stress can cause libido reduction, erectile dysfunction in men, and irregular menstrual cycles in women. Healthy sexual functioning depends on controlling stress and preserving hormonal balance.

To control sexual desire, arousal, responsiveness, and general sexual behavior, these hormones interact with neurotransmitters in the brain as well as with one another. Sexual health and function can be impacted by hormone imbalances, such as those found in disorders like polycystic ovarian syndrome (PCOS), hypo- or hyperthyroidism, or hormonal swings during menopause. Hormonal therapy may be used to treat some sexual health issues, but for individualized advice and treatment, it's crucial to speak with medical specialists.

Evolutionary Views of Human Sexuality:

By analyzing how evolutionary processes have impacted our sexual behaviors, wants, and preferences across time, evolutionary psychology provides important insights into understanding human sexuality. According to this viewpoint, a lot of characteristics of human sexuality can be linked to adaptive processes that developed to improve the chances of successful reproduction and survival.

1. Reproductive Imperatives: Evolutionary theory highlights the basic role that reproduction plays in determining sexual behavior. Sex serves primarily as a means of effective reproduction and the transfer of genetic material to offspring, according to evolutionary theory. From this angle, actions like choosing a partner, attracting attention, and investing in one's parents are seen as tactics meant to optimize reproductive fitness.

Evolutionary psychologists suggest that strategies for mate selection are impacted by evolved preferences that are favorable for successful reproduction. For example, because these characteristics indicate reproductive viability, men may show a preference for young appearance and fertility markers (such as clear skin and a healthy waist-to-hip ratio) in possible partners. However, when choosing a partner, women could give preference to characteristics related to wealth, safety, and parental involvement.

3. Sexual tactics hypothesis: According to this hypothesis, males and females have developed different reproductive tactics in order to maximize their chances of successful reproduction. According to theory, men choose to pursue mating strategies that are more immediate, concentrating on finding more partners in order to increase the likelihood that their genes would be passed on. Because pregnancy and childrearing involve a greater investment, women, on the other hand, typically take a more selective approach, prioritizing quality over quantity when choosing a partner.

4. Parental Investment: The idea of parental investment—which is the time, effort, and resources people devote to their children—is emphasized by evolutionary viewpoints. Women are generally more choosy in their mate selection process because they invest more in gestation and breastfeeding and are therefore better able to offer resources and support for their offspring. In order to secure fatherhood and attract partners, men may also participate in competitive behaviors.

5. Reproductive Strategies: Evolutionary psychologists also look at how different situations and civilizations use reproduction. Mating preferences, timing of reproduction, and family arrangements can be influenced by various factors, including but not limited to socioeconomic level, availability of resources, social norms, and environmental circumstances.

6. Sexual Jealousy and Mate Guarding: According to evolutionary theories, sexual jealousy and mate guarding behaviors have developed as defense mechanisms against factors that could jeopardize reproductive fitness, such as betrayal or diminished mate value. Differential reproductive risks may be reflected in men's greater worry for sexual infidelity and women's greater sensitivity to emotional infidelity.

7. Sexual Orientation Evolution: From an adaptive perspective, evolutionary viewpoints also investigate the genesis and variation of sexual orientation. Even non-reproductive sexual activities may indirectly benefit genetic relations, according to theories like kin selection and inclusive fitness, which may explain why there is still heterogeneity in sexual orientation among populations.

8. Challenges and Criticisms: Although evolutionary theories offer important new perspectives on human sexuality, there are some drawbacks to them. Opponents contend that evolutionary explanations could perpetuate gender stereotypes, oversimplify complicated behaviors, and ignore individual and cultural heterogeneity. Furthermore, sexual orientations and identities outside reproductive purposes are not taken into account by evolutionary theories.

To sum up, the framework provided by evolutionary perspectives on sexuality helps us comprehend the evolutionary history and adaptive roles of human sexual behaviors and desires. Evolutionary psychology advances our knowledge of the intricacies of human sexuality by examining how natural selection has influenced our mating behaviors, reproductive instincts, and social dynamics.

The influence of genetics on sexual orientation:

It is well-established, although the exact mechanisms and genetic components influencing this tendency are still being studied and clarified. In relation to genetics and sexual orientation, the following points are crucial:

1. Complexity of Sexual Orientation: A variety of genetic, hormonal, environmental, and social factors can impact a person's sexual orientation. The term "gender orientation" describes a person's persistent pattern of romantic, sexual, and emotional attraction to people who identify as either heterosexual, gay, bisexual, or neither of the aforementioned genders.

2. Family and Twin investigations: A hereditary component to sexual orientation is suggested by research investigations, including family and twin studies. In comparison to fraternal twins, who typically share 50% of their DNA, identical twins, who have almost identical genetic makeup, had higher concordance rates for sexual orientation, according to these research. This points to a hereditary component to sexual orientation, but it's crucial to remember that contextual influences also matter.

3. Putative Candidate Genes and Genetic Markers: Studies on genetics have revealed putative candidate genes and genetic markers connected to sexual orientation. Genes related to brain development, hormone control, and neurotransmitter pathways that may affect sexual desire and identity are frequently the subject of these investigations. Still, research is being done to better understand the precise genetic components and how they interact.

Prenatal Hormonal Factors: Exposure to androgen hormones (such as testosterone) during important fetal development stages has been linked to the development of sexual orientation. Hormone variations or sensitivity to hormones during pregnancy may have an impact on the development of the brain and the ensuing patterns of sexual identity and attraction.

5. Polygenic and Multifactorial Model: In addition to social and environmental factors, sexual orientation is probably impacted by a number of small-effect genetic factors. Sexual orientation is thought to be determined by a complex interaction between genetic and non-genetic variables rather than by a single gene or genetic variant, according to this polygenic and multifactorial concept.

6. Genetic Diversity and Variation: People with different sexual orientations experience a range of identities and attractions. Sexual orientation is diverse and exists along a continuum. The diversity of sexual orientations found within communities is a result of genetic variation and diversity, underscoring the complexity of human sexuality.

7. Ethical Issues and Social Consequences: Exploring the genetics of sexual orientation presents ethical questions about consent, privacy, discrimination, and stigma. Such study must be carried out in an ethical manner that upholds each person's autonomy and rights. The results must be used responsibly to further acceptance and understanding.

In conclusion, while genetics has an impact on sexual orientation, this influence is limited to one aspect of a complicated and multidimensional feature. To completely understand the genetic components of sexual orientation formation and how they interact with developmental and environmental factors, more research is required.

CHAPTER THREE

Sexual Development And Psychology:

Sexuality and psychological development are closely related, as different psychological processes have an impact on how relationships, beliefs, actions, and sexual identities are formed throughout life. Important details about sexuality and psychological development are as follows:

1. Early Childhood and Exploration: - Infant and Toddler Years: In these early years, children start to become self-aware and curious about their body. As a natural part of learning about their body, they could touch their genitalia and engage in other self-exploration activities.
During the preschool years, children begin to learn about sexuality-related cultural norms, gender roles, and societal expectations. In order to establish the groundwork for future relationships, they might also start to develop emotional and attachment ties with their caretakers.

2. Middle Childhood and the Formation of Identity: - Gender Identity: The sensation of being male, female, or non-binary is developed during this crucial time in life. As they play and interact with others, children learn more about their gender and may investigate gender norms and stereotypes.
- Body Image and Self-Esteem: During this stage, messages concerning peer comparisons, body image ideals, and beauty standards may have an impact on body image problems. A healthy sexual development depends on having a positive body image and self-esteem.

3. Teenage Years and Puberty:
- Pubertal Changes: Physical changes linked to puberty, such as the emergence of secondary sexual traits like breast development in females and facial hair growth in males, characterize adolescence. Sexual maturity and increased interest in sexuality are influenced by hormonal changes.
- Exploration of Sexual Identity: Adolescents start to investigate their attraction to other sexual orientations and romantic feelings. Questioning, self-discovery, and

managing peer pressure and society expectations may all be part of this phase of exploring one's sexual identity.

Adolescents may partake in risky activities associated with their sexuality, including substance abuse, peer pressure, and experimenting with sexual activity. To encourage sound decision-making and risk mitigation, it is imperative to provide education, communication, and advice.

4. Young Adulthood and the Formation of close partnerships: - Dating Experiences and Sexual Exploration: Young adulthood is marked by the development of close partnerships. In romantic partnerships, people deal with concerns of consent, communication, trust, and sexual satisfaction.

Young adults also prioritize sexual health and well-being, including contraception, STI prevention, and reproductive choices. Promoting sexual well-being requires having access to thorough sexual education and healthcare services.

5. Continuity and Adult Development: - Long-Term Relationships: As people get older, they might get married or form other partnerships. Sexual contentment and relationship length are influenced by mutual satisfaction, communication, intimacy, and trust.

- Parenthood and Family Dynamics: Among the new sexual dynamics that parenting brings about are fertility, family planning, parenting responsibilities, and preserving intimacy within the framework of the family. Finding a balance between the demands of parenthood and intimate relationships requires open communication and flexibility.

6. Age and Sexual Health:

- Sexual Functioning: Menopause and andropause are two examples of how sexual functioning varies with age in women. The sexual health and pleasure of older persons can be influenced by psychological variables, lifestyle decisions, and healthcare interventions.

- Intimacy and Connection: Despite changes brought on by aging, older persons still yearn for emotional closeness, intimacy, and sexual fulfillment. Sexual well-being in later life is supported by positive attitudes regarding aging, communication, and adaptive techniques.

7. Social and Cultural Influences: - Societal Norms: These norms influence how people view sexuality, gender roles, sexual orientation, and relationships. They also affect attitudes and expectations about these topics. These cultural standards differ and can impact how each person experiences sexuality.
- Media and Technology: Media, such as social media, digital platforms, and mainstream media, influence sexual norms, ideals, and practices. Navigating media impacts on sexuality requires media literacy and critical thinking abilities.

Psychological obstacles and Assistance: - Sexual Health Issues: People may encounter psychological obstacles associated with sexual health, such as intimacy worries, body image problems, sexual trauma, and sexual dysfunctions. Interventions and coping mechanisms for dealing with these issues are provided via counseling, therapy, and support programs.
- LGBTQ+ Identity: People with a variety of sexual orientations and gender identities could face particular psychological difficulties in relation to discrimination, stigma, coming out, and acceptance of their identities. Mental health and well-being are enhanced by LGBTQ+ accepting therapy and community support.

In summary, biological, psychological, social, and cultural variables all have an impact on the interwoven processes of psychological development and sexuality, which change over the course of a person's life. In order to facilitate healthy sexual development, educated decision-making, and supportive environments for people's sexual identities and relationships, it is imperative that these developmental stages and psychological dynamics be understood.

Development of Sexuality Throughout Life.

Throughout life, sexual development is characterized by a range of biological, psychological, and social transformations that impact people's perspectives, actions, and encounters with sexuality. This is a summary of how sexual development occurs at various phases of life:

First Childhood and Early Years (0–5 Years):

- Curiosity about one's body and sensation-seeking are the main ways that sexuality is manifested in infancy and early childhood.

- Youngsters start to get a basic awareness of gender identity and the distinctions between men and women.

- Caregivers are essential in educating children about body parts, limits, and personal safety at the proper age.

2. Intermediate Childhood (ages 6 to 11):

- Middle childhood is a time when curiosity and exploration of relationships and sexuality continue.

- Youngsters learn more about cultural expectations surrounding sexuality, gender roles, and social conventions.

This period may see the start of age-appropriate education regarding consent, reproductive health, and puberty.

3. Teenage years (12–18):

- Growth spurts, the emergence of secondary sexual traits, and hormonal variations are some of the physical changes that occur during puberty, which is a crucial stage of sexual development.

Teens who are navigating their sexual identity, orientation, and love relationships are more attracted to, curious about, and exploratory of sexual matters.

It becomes imperative to provide comprehensive sexual education covering subjects like STIs, consent, body image, puberty, and healthy relationships.

Adolescents are prone to risk-taking activities, such as peer pressure, experimentation, and early sexual engagement. In order to encourage risk minimization and well-informed decision-making, assistance and guidance are essential.

Fourth Stage of Life (19–39 Years Old):

- The early years of adulthood are a time for intimate sexual exploration and the development of relationships.

People become more aware of their sexual identity, interests, and values; these factors impact partner choice and sexual activity.

As people navigate personal relationships and reproductive choices, sexual health, contraception, family planning, and STI prevention become priorities.

Healthy sexual functioning and well-being are mostly dependent on communication, trust, closeness, and sexual satisfaction.

5. Middle Adulthood (Age Range of 40–59):

Although people may undergo changes in sexual desire, arousal, and functioning owing to aging, hormonal shifts, and life upheavals, middle adulthood is characterized by stability in sexual identity and relationships.

- In long-term relationships, maintaining sexual fulfillment and connection requires emotional intimacy, communication, and adaptability to physical changes.

- Parenting duties, intimacy within the family, and fertility are all factors that might affect how a person expresses and prioritizes their sexuality.

6. Late Adulthood (over the age of 60):

Intimacy, connection, and sexual fulfillment are sought after by older individuals as their sexual development continues until late adulthood.

- Age-related changes, such as erectile function, sexual response, lubrication, and menopause in women and men, might impact sexual desire and erectile function.

- Supporting later-life sexual well-being and happiness includes open communication, adaptability, and medical interventions (such as hormone therapy and sexual counseling).

- Satisfying sexual relationships in later adulthood are facilitated by emotional connection, mutual respect, and shared experiences.

Biological (hormones, aging), psychological (identity formation, self-esteem), social (cultural norms, relationships), and environmental (education, healthcare access) factors all have an impact on how an individual experiences sexual development over the course of their lifetime. Promoting healthy attitudes, behaviors, and relationships throughout life's stages is made easier by having an understanding of the various pathways of sexual development.

The Influence of Culture and Family on Sexual Beliefs:

Family and culture have a big impact on sexual ideas because they are important social forces that pass down sexual norms, values, and attitudes from one generation to the next. The following main ideas illustrate how culture and family influence sexual beliefs:

1. Family Values and Communication: Families are the main socialization factors that influence an individual's sexual orientation-related attitudes, beliefs, and behaviors.
- The way that sexuality is viewed, addressed, and controlled in the family setting is influenced by religious convictions, cultural customs, and family values.
- Informed decision-making and healthy sexual development are supported by open and encouraging dialogue about sexuality, relationships, consent, and reproductive health within families.

2. Cultural Norms and Expectations: - Within a particular country or group, cultural norms establish what behaviors, roles, and sexual displays are acceptable and unacceptable.
People's conceptions of sexual identity, relationships, and intimacy are influenced by cultural ideals surrounding gender roles, sexual orientation, marriage, families, and modesty.
Puberty, marriage, and childbirth are examples of important sexuality-related milestones that may be marked by cultural customs, ceremonies, and rites of passage.

3. Religious and Moral Influences: - Sexual ideas and behaviors are frequently greatly influenced by religious convictions and moral lessons.
- Diverse theological traditions hold differing views on issues including sexual ethics, LGBTQ+ rights, abortion, contraception, and premarital sex.
- Religious teachings can offer direction, moral principles, and frameworks for marriage, faithfulness, sexual conduct, and family life.

4. Parental guidance and role modeling: - Children and teenagers look to parents and other caregivers as role models and sources of information regarding sexuality. Children's views, beliefs, and degree of comfort with sexuality are shaped by their parents' attitudes, behaviors, and conversations regarding relationships, sex, consent, and sexual health.
- Respect for the diversity of sexual identities and beliefs, healthy sexual development, and communication skills are all influenced by positive parental supervision, education, and support.

5. Media and Cultural Influences: Entertainment, advertising, literature, and digital media all have an impact on how society views sexuality and the standards and values that surround it.
- Media portrayals of gender, sexuality, relationships, and beauty standards can either support or contradict preconceived notions and ideas.
- Critical thinking abilities, media literacy, and conversations regarding media influences are crucial for understanding and interpreting societal messages regarding sexuality.

6. Education and Awareness Programs: - Community projects, formal education programs, and awareness campaigns all contribute to the advancement of LGBTQ+ inclusion, consent education, and sexual health education.
- Accurate knowledge, abilities, and resources provided by comprehensive sexual education enable people to make wise choices regarding their sexual rights, relationships, and well-being.
Approaches to sexual education that are inclusive and culturally sensitive embrace a range of identities, values, and perspectives within various familial and cultural contexts.

7. Social Change and Advocacy: - Social movements, advocacy initiatives, and legislative modifications aid in the fight against sexuality-related stigma, discrimination, and inequality.
- Cultural advances toward diversity in sexual identities and views, acceptance, and inclusivity support sexual rights, individuality, and well-being for people from all walks of life.

In conclusion, sexual attitudes, values, and actions are greatly influenced by family and culture. Families and communities can help to promote positive sexual development, healthy relationships, and respect for varied sexual ideas and identities by encouraging open communication, cultural sensitivity, education, and activism.

Forming a Sexual Identity:

People establish their perception of their own sexual orientation, attraction, wants, and sexuality-related beliefs through a complicated and varied process called sexual identity formation. Factors related to biology, psychology, society, and culture all impact this process. The following are essential details regarding the creation of sexual identity:

1. Exploration and Awareness: The adolescent and early adult years are crucial for investigating and realizing one's sexual identity.
-An individual's understanding of their sexual orientation (heterosexual, gay, bisexual, asexual, etc.) may be aided by fantasies, experiences, and desires.

This process of discovery involves self-examination, introspection, and social engagement with romantic interests and peers.

The social and cultural context of an individual can greatly impact their perception and interpretation of their sexual identity. This includes cultural and societal conventions, beliefs, and attitudes about sexuality.
"- People's comfort level and preparedness to accept their sexual identity can be influenced by acceptance, stigma, and prejudice associated to various sexual orientations.
Positive development of one's sexual identity can be aided by exposure to a range of viewpoints, positive role models, and encouraging circumstances.

The coming out process, which starts with self-acceptance and acknowledgment, is the act of revealing one's gender identity or sexual orientation to both oneself and other people.
"- Coming out can be difficult on an internal level and may involve worries about safety, fear of rejection, and stigma associated with LGBTQ+ identities in certain settings. Individuals can receive assistance throughout the coming out process from supportive relationships, LGBTQ+ networks, and resources (such as counseling and support groups).

Identity labels such as gay, lesbian, bisexual, queer, and pansexual can be used by people to define their sexual orientation; however, other people prefer to identify as fluid or non-binary instead of using labels at all.

It is possible for sexual orientation to be fluid and to vary over time in response to shifting experiences, attractions, and self-perceptions.

- Accepting non-binary identities and fluidity adds to the complexity and diversity of sexual orientation within the LGBTQ+ community.

5. Intersectionality: - Aspects of identity such as gender identity, race, ethnicity, religion, socioeconomic status, and disability intersect with sexual identity.

"- Within LGBTQ+ communities and society at large, intersectionality affects people's experiences of privilege, marginalization, discrimination, and access to resources. Gaining an understanding of intersectionality is essential to fostering environments that are affirming and inclusive while respecting a range of sexual identities and life experiences.

Psychosocial Development: - Identity exploration, autonomy, closeness, and self-acceptance are all closely linked to the establishment of a sexual identity. According to Erik Erikson's psychological phases, sexual identity is a crucial component of the identity versus role uncertainty that occurs between adolescence and early adulthood.

7. Supportive Environments and Resources: - Key roles in promoting good sexual identity formation are played by supportive environments, such as families, schools, workplaces, healthcare settings, and communities.

Having access to resources, education, mental health treatments, and advocacy organizations that support LGBTQ+ people improves people's resilience and well-being while they are forming their identities.

In conclusion, the development of one's sexual identity is a dynamic and unique process impacted by a range of internal and external influences. It is crucial to establish inclusive, encouraging, and affirming settings in order to assist the development of healthy sexual identities and to uphold the rights, dignity, and acceptance of people of all gender identities and sexual orientations.

Psychological Difficulties Associated with Sexual Development:

An individual's emotional health, interpersonal connections, and general quality of life may be negatively impacted by psychological issues linked to sexual development at any point in their lives. These difficulties may arise from both internal (such as self-perception and identity exploration) and external (such as societal norms, stigma, and trauma) sources. Key psychological issues pertaining to sexual development include as follows:

1. Identity Investigation and Perplexity:

- Young adults and adolescents frequently go through identity discovery and may be unsure of their gender identity, sexual orientation, or place in relationships.

Stress, worry, and self-doubt can result from identity uncertainty, which can be exacerbated by internal conflicts, external pressures, and a lack of supportive surroundings.

2. Personality and Self-Regard:

Self-esteem and sexual confidence can be impacted by body image issues, such as unhappiness with one's physical appearance or sexual performance.

- Gender norms, media depictions, and societal standards of beauty may all contribute to body image problems, which can affect intimate and satisfying sexual experiences in relationships

3. Impaired Sexual Orientation:

- Physiological, psychological, or relational variables can give rise to sexual dysfunctions such as low libido, orgasmic disorders, early ejaculation, and erectile dysfunction.

- Sexual dysfunctions can cause distress and decreased sexual satisfaction. These dysfunctions can be attributed to interpersonal difficulties, performance anxiety, past sexual trauma, and underlying medical disorders.

4: Trauma and Sexual Abuse

- Past sexual assault, abuse, or trauma experiences can have a significant psychological impact on a person's ability to develop and function sexually.

- Individuals who have experienced trauma may struggle with post-traumatic stress disorder, building healthy relationships, intimacy concerns, trust issues, and dissociation during sexual activities.

5. Relationship and Intimacy Issues:

It can be difficult to establish and maintain close relationships, especially for those who are juggling concerns with their sexual orientation, communication difficulties, trust issues, or cultural differences.

Relationship problems, mental pain, loneliness, and unfulfilled sexual urges can result from adultery, lack of intimacy, and mismatched sexual appetites.

6. Prejudice and Stigma:

Stress and psychological discomfort among minorities are exacerbated by stigma, discrimination, and prejudice pertaining to sexual orientation, gender identity, and various sexualities.

- The mental health and general well-being of LGBTQ+ people may be negatively impacted by social rejection, bullying, harassment, and internalized homophobia and transphobia.

7. Acceptance of Sexual Orientation and Gender Identity:

- Self-acceptance, societal acceptance, and familial acceptance can be difficult for those who are exploring or coming to terms with their gender identity or sexual orientation.

Feelings of alienation, guilt, and internal strife can result from rejection, invalidation, or a lack of support from friends, family, or communities.

8. Conflicts between Cultures and Religions:

- Individuals' personal values, wants, or identities may clash with cultural conventions, religious views, and societal expectations surrounding sexuality.

Psychological tension and identity problems can arise when cultural or religious convictions are balanced with acceptance of one's identity, sexual expression, and autonomy.

9. Insufficient Resources and Education:

People's capacity to address sexual difficulties, seek help, and make educated decisions may be hampered by a lack of access to comprehensive sexual education, mental health treatments, and LGBTQ+-affirming resources.

- People may be discouraged from seeking professional treatment, which could result in unmet psychological needs, due to stigma around sexuality, mental health, and help-seeking behaviors.

It takes a comprehensive approach to address psychological issues surrounding sexual development. This approach must include mental health support, education, advocacy for LGBTQ+ rights, trauma-informed care, and the creation of inclusive environments that promote acceptance, dignity, and well-being for people of all gender identities and sexual orientations.

CHAPTER FOUR

Sexual Desire and Arousal:

Fundamental components of human sexuality, sexual arousal and desire are the physiological, psychological, and emotional reactions that support sexual interest, pleasure, and closeness. Key ideas on sexual arousal and desire are as follows:

1. What Sexual Arousal and Desire Mean?

- Sexual Arousal: The term describes the body's and mind's reaction to sexual stimuli. It includes physical manifestations like genital engorgement (a male erection, a female vaginal lubrication), elevated heart rate, heightened sensory awareness, and a readiness for sexual activity.
- Sexual want: Sexual want, sometimes referred to as libido, is the motivational, affective, and cognitive components of sexual interest and attraction. It involves the anticipation of sexual experiences as well as feelings of yearning and interest.

2. Elements Affecting Desire and Sexual Arousal:

- Biological Elements:
- Hormonal Influences: The hormones testosterone, estrogen, and other ones influence sexual arousal, libido, and reproductive processes.
- Neurotransmitters: Dopamine, serotonin, and endorphins are neurotransmitters that influence motivation, reward, and pleasure systems in the brain. They also play a role in arousal and sexual desire.
- Genital reaction: In reaction to sexual stimulation, the body's blood flow to the genital organs, lubrication, and erectile tissue (the penis in men, the clitoris in women) are all affected.

- Aspects of Psychology:

The stimulation of the imagination and activation of pleasure centers in the brain can be achieved through sexual fantasies, ideas, and mental imagery, which in turn can heighten arousal and desire.

- Emotional Connection: A partner's feelings of intimacy, trust, and attraction can heighten arousal and sexual desire.

- Anxiety and Mood: Negative psychological elements that might affect sexual arousal and desire include anxiety, despair, tension, exhaustion, and body image problems.

Factors related to society and environment:

The dynamics of relationships, including communication, trust, emotional intimacy, and mutual respect, all have an impact on a partner's sexual desire and fulfillment.

Cultural conventions, values, beliefs, media portrayals, and societal views regarding sexuality all have an impact on how people perceive and express their sexual desire.

- **Environmental Context:** Ambient cues (such as a romantic setting or sensual stimuli) and privacy, comfort, and safety can either increase or decrease sexual arousal and desire.

Development and Lifecycle Shifts: - Puberty and Adolescence: During puberty, hormonal changes lead to an increase in sexual desire and a heightened sense of sexual curiosity.

- Adulthood: Hormonal changes, challenges in life, the dynamics of relationships, and individual experiences can all cause fluctuations in sexual desire.

- Aging: In older persons, hormonal fluctuations, medical disorders, and age-related variables might impact sexual desire and performance.

3. Sexual Desire Types: - Spontaneous Desire: This type of desire is experienced by certain people and is defined by impulsive or sudden cravings for sexual activity without the need for particular cues or triggers.

- Responsive want: This type of sexual want is experienced by others, in which erotic cues, physical touch, or closeness with a partner trigger feelings of sexual interest and arousal.

- Mixed Desire: Certain individuals may exhibit a blend of responsive and impulsive desire, with their sexual interest fluctuating according to both internal and external circumstances.

4. Disparities in Desire and Sexual Dysfunction:

Sexual Dysfunction: Disorders affecting the ability to experience or sustain sexual arousal, desire, or satisfaction include anorgasmia, erectile dysfunction, and hypoactive sexual desire disorder (HSDD).

Desire Discrepancy: Differences in sexual desire levels between partners can cause problems with communication, intimacy, and relationship satisfaction.

5. Improving Desire and Sexual Arousal:

- Communication: Honest and transparent dialogue on fantasies, sexual preferences, boundaries, and desires promotes understanding, intimacy, and mutual fulfillment.

- Emotional Connection: Developing affectionate gestures, trust, and emotional intimacy in partnerships heightens arousal and sexual desire.

- Sensual Stimulation: Intense physical contact, such as kissing, cuddling, massaging, and foreplay, can increase arousal and the desire for sex.

- Self-Care and Well-Being: Maintaining general health (physical, emotional, and mental), controlling stress, giving self-care a high priority, and attending to any underlying sexual issues all contribute to sexual well-being and desire.

Support from professionals: Seeking advice, evaluation, and therapy for sexual dysfunctions or relationship problems from therapists, medical professionals, or sex therapists can enhance sexual functioning and satisfaction.

Individuals and couples can better manage their sexual encounters, increase closeness, and handle any obstacles or worries by having a thorough understanding of the complex nature of sexual arousal and desire. Building happy and healthy sexual relationships requires a lot of communication, education, self-awareness, and respect for one another.

Understanding Sexual Arousal Patterns:

Recognizing the various ways people experience and react to sexual stimuli, such as bodily sensations, thoughts, emotions, and environmental cues, is essential to understanding sexual arousal patterns. Many factors, including biological, psychological, social, and cultural ones, might have an impact on an individual's sexual arousal patterns. Knowing sexual arousal patterns is important for the following reasons:

1. Individual Variability: – Sexual arousal patterns vary greatly depending on the individual, including intensity, duration, triggers, and preferences.
. When exposed to particular cues (such as visual, aural, or tactile ones), some people may become sexually aroused quickly, while others may need more time or particular circumstances.
. A person's arousal patterns can be influenced by experiences from the past, associations that have been learned, fantasies, emotional moods, and physical health.

2. Different Types of Sexual Arousal: - Spontaneous Arousal: Not requiring conscious effort or outside stimuli, spontaneous arousal arises naturally. Symptoms include elevated sensitivity to sexual cues, respiratory abnormalities, rapid genital arousal, and elevated heart rate.
The third type of sexual arousal is called responsive arousal, which occurs when a person experiences sexual excitement in reaction to erotic stimuli, physical contact, sexual thoughts, or close relationships.
Contextual Arousal: Responses to environmental stimuli, interpersonal dynamics, privacy, comfort, and emotional connection can all influence an individual's level of arousal.

3. Physiological Reactions: - Genital Reaction: Penile tumescence, or the erection in men, and vaginal lubrication, or the engorgement of the clitoris and vaginal walls in women, are examples of physiological reactions common to sexual desire.

Arousal causes the autonomic nervous system to become activated, which in turn causes dilated pupils, an accelerated heart rate, increased blood flow to the genital organs, and an increased level of sensory awareness.

Arousal can be heightened by sexual fantasies, mental imagery, and erotic ideas, which activate the brain's reward centers, release dopamine, and heighten subjective pleasure. These are the cognitive and emotional influences that influence arousal.
- Emotional Connection: Desire and arousal for sexual activity can be enhanced by feelings of emotional connection, trust, attractiveness, and affection toward a spouse.
Psychological States: A person's capacity to feel arousal and be responsive to sexual stimuli can be influenced by their mood, stress level, anxiety, level of relaxation, emotional well-being, and distraction.

Environmental and sensory factors: - Environmental Cues: By fostering an intimate atmosphere, physical surroundings such as lighting, music, ambiance, and privacy can affect sexual arousal.
- Sensory Stimulation: Sexual arousal reactions can be elicited by a variety of sensory stimuli, including touch, kisses, caresses, erotic words, visual stimuli (such as pornographic images, movies), and aural signals (such as whispers, groans).

6. Social and Cultural Influences: - Cultural Norms: An individual's perception and reaction to sexual stimuli are influenced by their cultural values, taboos, and views about sexuality.
Social messages: People's conceptions of arousal, desire, and sexual expression are shaped by media portrayals, cultural norms, gender roles, and sexual scripts.

7. Variability Over Time: - Many life phases, hormonal variations (such as the menstrual cycle and menopause), interpersonal dynamics, stressors, and physical health changes can all have an impact on arousal patterns, which can then shift over time and in context.

Acquiring an understanding of one's own inclinations, triggers, and reactions to sexual stimuli necessitates self-awareness, conversation, and research. To improve intimacy, sexual satisfaction, and understanding between partners, relationships should foster an open and supportive environment where people feel comfortable sharing their fantasies, desires, and arousal patterns.

The psychological and emotional dimensions of sexual attraction:

Individuals' sentiments, desires, and reactions to possible partners or stimuli are influenced by intricate psychological and emotional processes associated with sexual attraction. These factors have a big impact on how romantic and sexual relationships develop because they have an impact on partner choice, attraction dynamics, and emotional ties. Key information regarding the mental and emotional components of sexual desire is as follows:

1. Psychological Factors: - Personal Preferences: Depending on their physical characteristics, personality traits, beliefs, hobbies, IQ, sense of humor, and communication style, people have different preferences and attraction triggers.
- Familiarity and Similarity: People are more attracted to each other when they have similar attitudes, views, backgrounds, and life experiences because they feel more at ease, connected, and understood by others who share their interests.
Physical Attractiveness: Although opinions of attractiveness are arbitrary and shaped by culture, physical attributes such as face symmetry, body proportions, grooming, and sense of style can affect an individual's first attraction.
Psychological compatibility: This type of compatibility, which includes communication abilities, empathy, emotional intelligence, and conflict resolution approaches, promotes emotional closeness and connection, which in turn leads to long-lasting attraction.
- Sexual Chemistry: In intimate relationships, chemistry, similar sexual interests, and sexual compatibility all play a role in arousing and attracting sexual desire.

2. Aspects of the Emotions: - Emotional Connection: Mutual understanding, emotional intimacy, trust, and vulnerability intensify emotional attraction and promote closeness and bonding in partnerships.
- Attachment Styles: According to attachment theory, people's attachment styles—such as secure, anxious, or avoidant—have an impact on how they develop emotional connections and feel attracted to others in relationships.

The initial phases of attraction are marked by powerful emotions, fixation, and a strong need for intimacy with the object of attraction. These feelings are commonly referred to as infatuation, limerence, or romantic idealization.
- Empathy and Compassion: These qualities build a sense of concern, validation, and emotional safety in relationships, which in turn contributes to attraction.
- Emotional Resonance: Partners' emotional connection and attraction are strengthened when they have emotional resonance, which is produced by shared experiences, values, and emotional reactions.

3. Dreams and Mental Imagery: - Fantasies related to sexuality: Dreams and mental imagery influence arousal, desire, and anticipation of sexual encounters, which contributes to sexual attraction.
- Erotic Thoughts: In partnerships, erotic ideas, fantasies, and thoughts about a partner can increase libido, closeness, and pleasure.
- Creativity and imagination: Imagination, creativity, and the capacity to picture shared experiences enhance sexual and emotional attraction, bringing excitement and freshness to partnerships.

4. Social and Cultural Influences: - Cultural Norms: How people perceive attraction, show romantic interest, and negotiate relationships is influenced by cultural norms, gender roles, and society ideals of romance.
The process of socialization involves how people comprehend attraction, beauty standards, and relationship dynamics through their encounters with peers, media, and social conventions.

5. Developmental Considerations: - Developmental Stages: Attraction patterns can differ between developmental stages, with adolescence, early adulthood, and later stages of life exhibiting distinct attraction preferences, priorities, and relationship objectives.
- Identity Development: Attraction, desire, and relationship dynamics are experienced differently by individuals depending on their sexual orientation, gender identity, and identity discovery.

6. Individual Development and Self-Awareness:
- Self-Discovery: When people become more cognizant of their needs, limits, values, and preferred types of relationships, they are better able to recognize and accept themselves, which in turn leads to the development of healthy attraction patterns.
- Emotional Intelligence: In partnerships, emotional intelligence abilities like self-control, empathy, and effective communication foster emotional connection, mutual understanding, and attraction.

7. expression and Consent: - Mutual Interest: The establishment of consensual and courteous relationships requires mutual interest, mutual attraction, and unambiguous expression of romantic or sexual interest.
- Boundaries and Consent: Managing closeness and attraction sensibly requires acknowledging and honoring mutual comfort and safety as well as respecting boundaries and getting consent.
To summarize, a range of factors, including cultural influences, self-awareness, emotional connection, personal preferences, and developmental concerns, contribute to the psychological and emotional components of sexual attraction. In order to navigate attraction, create wholesome relationships, and promote emotional closeness and fulfillment in romantic engagements, people need to understand these dynamics.

Individual Variations in Sexual Desire:

Individual differences in sexual desire are common, and a variety of factors, including biological, psychological, social, and environmental effects, can have an impact. The varying experiences, interests, and attitudes regarding sexuality are influenced by these variances in sexual desire. Key variations in sexual desire among people are as follows:

1. Libido Levels: - High Libido: Persistent thoughts of sex, intense cravings, and a strong enthusiasm in engaging in sexual activities are signs of a high libido in certain people.
- Low Libido: Some people may have lower libidos, or lower levels of sexual desire, as evidenced by fewer sex-related thoughts, less arousal cravings, and less interest in engaging in sexual activities.

2. How Often Do You Have Sexual Thoughts and Fantasies?
The frequency of thoughts pertaining to sex, sexual fantasies, and erotic imagery varies among individuals. While some people may think about their sexuality more often than others during the day, others might not.
- Intensity of Fantasies: Individuals' sexual fantasies differ in terms of their intensity and content, which is indicative of their own inclinations, desires, and dreams about their sexual encounters.

3. Adaptive versus Instinctive Want:
- Responsive Desire: Affected people may have responsive sexual desire, which is characterized by arousal and sexual interest sparked by certain stimuli such physical contact, sensual cues, or close relationships.
- Spontaneous Desire: Those who don't encounter specific triggers or stimuli may nevertheless have sudden impulses or drives for sexual action.

4. Impact of Hormonal Fluctuations: - Hormonal Influences: Changes in testosterone and estrogen levels, for example, can have an impact on arousal and sexual desire. Libido can be impacted by changes in the menstrual cycle,

pregnancy, the postpartum phase, menopause, or andropause (aging of the male genitalia).

Medical diseases and drugs: Libido and sexual desire can be affected by a number of medical diseases and drugs, including thyroid disorders, antidepressants, and hormonal imbalances.

5. Relationship Context: - Partner Influence: A romantic partner's presence and interactions might affect a person's desire for sex. Individual desire levels can be influenced by elements like sexual compatibility, emotional connection, communication, attraction, and relationship satisfaction.

- Duration of Relationship: Throughout a relationship, factors such as intimacy, novelty, routine, stress in life, and interpersonal dynamics can all have an impact on changes in sexual desire.

6. Psychological and Emotional Factors: - Stress and Mood: Negative psychological effects on sexual desire, such as weariness, melancholy, anxiety, and stress, might lower interest in sexual engagement.

- Emotional Connection: In relationships, feelings of emotional closeness, trust, affection, and understanding are associated with increased sexual desire and attraction.

- Self-Esteem and Body Image: While poor self-esteem or body dissatisfaction may have a detrimental effect on desire, positive body image, self-esteem, and self-confidence are linked to higher levels of sexual desire.

7. Societal and Cultural Influences: - Cultural Norms: People's views of sexual norms, sexual expression, and sexual desire are influenced by cultural values, beliefs, and attitudes around sexuality.

Gender Roles: Depending on cultural norms surrounding male and female sexuality, gender roles and expectations can influence how sexual desire is experienced and expressed.

8. Sexual Orientation and Identity: - LGBTQ+ Variability: Individuals belonging to a variety of sexual orientations and gender identities exhibit varying sexual desire patterns, which are indicative of variations in attraction, desires, and sexual experiences within the LGBTQ+ community.

Examining one's sexual orientation, gender identity, and sexual behaviors can have an impact on how one feels about their own experiences of sexual desire, pleasure, and fulfillment.

9. Developmental Changes: - Life Stages: Throughout life, a person's sexual desire may alter due to several factors such as hormone fluctuations, life transitions, relationship status, and personal development.
- Aging: Taking into account changes in hormones, age-related modifications in sexual functioning, and health issues that impact libido, sexual desire may vary with age.

Personal Values and Priorities: Differing sexual desires are influenced by a person's values, priorities, sex-related beliefs, and cultural upbringing. These factors also influence how an individual prefers intimacy, communication, consent, and relationship dynamics.
- Personal Boundaries: Individuals' ability to navigate sexual desire, set sexual boundaries, and express their needs and preferences in relationships is influenced by their respect for their own autonomy, consent, and personal boundaries.

It is necessary to acknowledge these complex elements in order to comprehend the diversity of sexual desire among people. Individual variations, preferences, and boundaries must also be respected in close relationships and sexual interactions. Respecting each person's distinct needs and desires while promoting healthy and fulfilling sexual experiences requires permission, communication, empathy, and understanding.

CHAPTER FIVE

Relationships, Love, and Intimacy:

The notions of love, intimacy, and relationships are interdependent and essential to interpersonal interactions and mental health. Below are comprehensive explanations of each of these components and how important they are to creating deep connections:

1. Love: Love is an emotion with many facets and complexities, encompassing passion, commitment, empathy, compassion, and attachment. Numerous types of love exist, and each one adds something special to relationships and interpersonal connections:

Romantic love is characterized by a strong emotional bond, longing, and attraction to a romantic partner. Passion, infatuation, desire, and admiration are common emotions associated with it.
- Love Within the Family: Love within the family is the connection and fondness that exists between siblings, parents and kids, and other family members. Care, support, loyalty, and a feeling of community define it.
- Platonic Love: This type of closeness and non-romantic, non-sexual love is exchanged between friends or associates. Mutual respect, understanding, and a strong emotional connection are all necessary.
- Self-Love: Also known as self-compassion, self-love is the awareness, respect, and care of one's own needs, limits, and general well-being. It has to do with accepting, valuing, and taking care of oneself.

Love is a motivating factor for emotional connection, fulfillment, and personal development in relationships. It affects attitudes, actions, priorities, and life decisions.

2. Intimacy: Intimacy is the closeness, emotional kinship, trust, and vulnerability that people in partnerships share. It includes a range of intimate relationships, all of which add complexity and complexities to the relationship:

- Emotional Intimacy: To develop a profound sense of comprehension, empathy, and connection, emotional intimacy entails expressing feelings, thoughts, concerns, dreams, and vulnerabilities with a partner.
- Physical Intimacy: This type of intimacy promotes intimacy, enjoyment, and connection between lovers through touch, affection, sexual activity, and nonverbal communication.
- Intellectual Intimacy: Fostering mental stimulation and connection via meaningful conversations, sharing of ideas, ideals, and intellectual activities, intellectual intimacy is all about this.
- Spiritual Intimacy: This type of intimacy deepens partnerships' feeling of purpose, shared meaning, and connection by involving the sharing of spiritual views, values, practices, and experiences.

The quality and resiliency of interpersonal ties are improved by intimacy, which promotes emotional stability, support, and relationship happiness.

Relationships: Whether they are platonic, family, romantic, or professional, relationships comprise the exchanges, dynamics, and ties that exist between people. Important elements of wholesome and satisfying partnerships consist of:

- Communication: To effectively communicate, one must practice active listening, empathy, honesty, transparency, and the courteous expressing of one's needs as well as thoughts and feelings.
- Trust: Mutual respect, honesty, integrity, constancy, and dependability are the foundations of trust. It is the cornerstone of strong and safe relationships.
- Respect: In order to be respectful, people must value one another's viewpoints, limits, independence, and uniqueness. It entails respecting diversity, empathetic behavior, and refraining from criticism or judgment.
Encouragement: Social, pragmatic, and emotional support are provided by supportive connections at difficult times, life changes, achievements, and everyday encounters.

- Boundaries: In partnerships, well-established boundaries create autonomy, safety, and clear expectations. They also foster emotional stability and mutual respect.
- Shared Values and Objectives: Harmony, compatibility, and mutual development are nurtured in partnerships when values, objectives, priorities, and lifestyle choices are in alignment.
- Conflict Resolution: Effective conflict resolution techniques, such compromise, empathy, active listening, and problem-solving, help to settle disputes and advance harmonious relationships.

It takes work, empathy, communication, and a dedication to learning, growth, and relational fulfillment to cultivate healthy relationships.

In conclusion, relationships, love, and intimacy all play crucial roles in the development of emotional ties, personal development, and overall wellbeing. Building meaningful and satisfying relationships with people requires developing these qualities, which include self-awareness, communication, empathy, trust-building, and mutual respect.

The Psychology of Love:

This field of study covers a broad spectrum of feelings, actions, thought processes, and biological aspects that influence romantic attraction, intimacy, attachment, and relationship dynamics. The phenomena of love is intricate and multidimensional, and it has been thoroughly examined from a variety of psychological angles. Key ideas in the psychology of love are as follows:

1. Types of Love: - Passionate Love: comprised of strong feelings, a strong desire for intimacy with a romantic partner, and physical attraction. Feelings of arousal, excitement, and yearning are its defining characteristics.

   - Companionate Love: The foundations of companionate love include emotional intimacy, mutual respect, friendship, and trust. Warmth, affection, camaraderie, and enduring dedication are among its components.

   - Attachment Love: This concept, which emphasizes emotional ties, comfort, and security in partnerships, is based on attachment theory. It entails looking for a partner's closeness and support as well as trust and reliability.

   - Self-Love: Another name for self-compassion is self-love, which is the positive regard, acceptance, and nurturing of one's own needs, limits, and well-being. It has to do with accepting, valuing, and taking care of oneself.

2. Biological and Neurochemical Aspects: - Neurotransmitters: Dopamine, serotonin, and oxytocin are examples of neurotransmitters that are involved in pleasure, bonding, romantic attraction, and reward processing. Excitation and pleasure are linked to dopamine, mood and wellbeing are regulated by serotonin, and connection and bonding are encouraged by oxytocin.

   The influence of hormones, namely testosterone, estrogen, and vasopressin, on sexual desire, attraction, and attachment behaviors is a topic of discussion. Estrogen influences emotional bonding, vasopressin is involved in social attachment and pair bonding, while testosterone is connected to desire and arousal.

3. Attachment Theory: - John Bowlby and Mary Ainsworth developed attachment theory, which postulates that early attachment experiences with caregivers shape an

individual's attachment styles and patterns of behavior in romantic relationships as an adult.

- Secure Attachment: People who have secure attachment styles typically perceive the good in other people and themselves, are at ease in close quarters, and actively seek out companionship and connection.

- Anxious Attachment: People with this attachment style may be clingy or reliant in relationships, dread rejection, and want for confirmation and assurance.

The avoidant attachment style is characterized by a preference for independence, a fear of intimacy or vulnerability, difficulties expressing feelings, and a reluctance to ask for help.

4. The theory of love is the Robert Sternberg Triangular Theory of Love. According to this idea, love is comprised of three elements: commitment (the decision to stay in the relationship over the long term) and passion (physical attraction and desire). Intimacy is defined as emotional closeness and connection. There are several kinds of love that arise from different mixtures of these elements: high intimacy and passion in romantic love; high intimacy and commitment in companionate love; and balanced intimacy, passion, and commitment in consummate love.

The theories of evolution: According to evolutionary psychologists, attraction and love are adaptive mechanisms that have developed to support social bonding, mating, and reproduction. Romantic attraction and partner choice are influenced by ideas like reproductive strategy, parental investment, mate preferences, and sexual selection.

5. Cognitive and Emotional Processes: - Idealization and Positive Illusions: In the initial phases of romantic love, people tend to idealize their partners, see them as perfect, and ignore any imperfections or bad attributes. Sensationalism, exhilaration, and romantic idealization are fueled by positive illusions.

- Attachment and Bonding: In relationships, shared experiences, emotional bonding, trust, and vulnerability strengthen emotional connection and attachment. Sensations of safety, closeness, and contentment in relationships are nurtured by secure attachment.

6. Social and Cultural Influences: People's conceptions, expressions, and experiences of love and romance are shaped by society expectations, media portrayals, cultural norms, values, and beliefs. How love is understood and expressed in various cultural contexts is influenced by cultural differences in mate preferences, relationship dynamics, and expressions of love.
"- The expectations, definitions of love, and patterns of relationships in modern societies are influenced by societal developments, including changes in gender roles, family structures, and social standards.

Developmental Considerations: - Life experiences, relationship histories, developmental stages, and personal development all have an impact on how love and attachment patterns change throughout the course of a person's lifetime.
   - Adolescence: While navigating identity development and peer connections, adolescents encounter strong emotions, crushes, and romantic attraction explorations.
   - Adulthood: Romantic relationships in adulthood entail closer emotional ties, dedication, and intimacy as well as long-term compatibility, common objectives, and mutual development.
   - Later Life: As we age, our needs for intimacy, companionship, emotional support, and caregiving change along with our love and attachment patterns.
8. Characteristics of Love and Relationships:
      Communication: Good communication techniques are necessary for understanding, emotional connection, and positive relationship dynamics. These techniques include active listening, empathy, validation, and dispute resolution.
   - Faith and Adherence Relational security and emotional closeness are fostered by trustworthiness, consistency, reliability, and dedication to the partnership.
   - Mutual Respect: Respectful conduct, upholding autonomy, individuality, and limits, as well as demonstrating empathy and validation, all support mutual respect and the fulfillment of relationships.
   - Conflict Resolution: Harmony in relationships is fostered by constructive conflict resolution techniques like compromise, negotiation, and problem-solving.
   - Self-Awareness and Personal Development: Self-awareness, self-reflection, emotional control, and personal development improve people's capacity to interact in satisfying, healthy relationships, comprehend their own needs and preferences, and positively influence relational dynamics.

To summarize, the study of love psychology takes into account several factors such as biological, cognitive, emotional, social, cultural, and developmental aspects that impact romantic attraction, intimacy, attachment, and relationship dynamics. Gaining knowledge about these intricate procedures advances our understanding of the nature of love, the development of meaningful relationships, and the elements that support resilience, well-being, and relational happiness.

Relationship dynamics and attachment theory:

Relationship dynamics, emotional ties, and attachment styles are all better understood by applying attachment theory, which was created by John Bowlby and then extended by Mary Ainsworth and others. It focuses on how early interactions with caregivers mold people's attachment patterns, which then affects their intimacy and relational dynamics as adults. An in-depth examination of attachment theory and its consequences for relationship dynamics may be found here:

1. Important Attachment Theory Concepts:
- Attachment Bonds: Later social and emotional development is based on the emotional relationship and connection that develops between infants and caregivers. This bond is known as attachment.
- Secure Base: Infants can explore their surroundings and form a sense of trust and security by having caregivers provide them with safety, comfort, and support.
Internal working models are mental images of oneself, other people, and interpersonal connections that are developed as a result of early experiences with attachment. In adult relationships, these role models have an impact on behaviors, expectations, and beliefs.
- Attachment Styles: Based on the interplay between caregiver responsiveness and child demands, attachment theory distinguishes four main attachment styles:
- Secure Attachment: People with a secure attachment style are at ease in close quarters, have faith in others, ask for help when they need it, and perceive both themselves and other people favorably.
- Anxious-Preoccupied Attachment: People who are anxiously attached wish for intimacy, worry about their relationships, dread rejection or abandonment, and may act needy or clinging.
- Avoidant Attachment: People with this attachment style may avoid emotional expression or proximity in relationships, dread intimacy or vulnerability, and value independence.

- Disorganized Attachment: This condition, which is brought on by inconsistent or traumatic caregiving experiences, manifests as contradicting behaviors, confusion, and trouble controlling emotions and interpersonal interactions.

2. The Impact of Relationship Dynamics on Attachment Styles:
- Partner Selection: People frequently look for partners whose attachment styles are similar to or complementary to their own. This might result in compatibility or possible difficulties because of attachment expectations and demands.
- Communication Patterns: In relationships, attachment styles affect how people communicate, resolve conflicts, express their emotions, and be responsive.
- Emotional Intimacy: People with secure attachment styles typically have greater emotional closeness, trust, and fulfillment in their relationships, which promotes candid dialogue, understanding, and cooperation.
- Relationship Satisfaction: Secure attachment types are associated with greater stability, resilience, and relationship satisfaction, while insecure attachment styles may exacerbate problems, disputes, and discontent in relationships.
- Conflict and Resolution: Anxious attachment can cause increased sensitivity to envy, rejection, and conflicts; on the other hand, avoidant attachment can cause emotional detachment, problem minimization, and trouble resolving interpersonal conflicts.
- Effects of Early Life Experiences: People's adult attachment patterns and interpersonal dynamics are shaped by their early life experiences with attachment and providing care. In general, stable childhood attachments support stable adult attachments and positive interpersonal dynamics.

3. Modifying Attachment Patterns: - Therapeutic Interventions: Attachment-based treatments attempt to enhance communication skills, relationship satisfaction, emotional regulation, and attachment security. Examples of these therapies include Emotionally Focused Therapy (EFT) and attachment-focused interventions.
- Reflection and Self-Awareness: These activities can support relationship behaviors that are healthy and foster personal development by examining attachment styles, identifying triggers, and reflecting on relational dynamics.
- Emotional regulation and mindfulness: These practices, along with self-soothing methods, can assist people in managing attachment-related phobias, anxieties, and insecurities in interpersonal relationships.

- Relationship Education: Workshops, counseling, and relationship education programs offer techniques, tactics, and insights into healthy relationship dynamics, productive communication, handling conflict, and creating stable attachments.

4. Taking Context and Culture Into Account:
Cultural influences shape attachment patterns, relationship ideals, and communication techniques in a variety of cultural situations. These include cultural norms, values, family dynamics, and societal expectations.
- Interpersonal Context: Interpersonal aspects that foster emotional connection and relational happiness, such as trust, reciprocity, empathy, validation, and reciprocal support, have an impact on relationship dynamics.

In essence, attachment theory provides a framework for comprehending how people's attachment patterns, beliefs, and behaviors in adult relationships are shaped by their early attachment experiences. The development of healthy, satisfying relationships and the promotion of attachment security and intimacy depend heavily on relational skills, effective communication, emotional control, and awareness of attachment patterns.

Intimacy Development in Romantic Relationship:

The development of intimacy is an essential component of romantic partnerships as it promotes emotional bonding, mutual trust, and closeness between couples. Emotional, physical, intellectual, and spiritual intimacy are only a few of the facets that comprise intimacy. These are some methods and techniques to improve intimacy in love relationships:

1. Effective Communication: - Active Listening: Show your partner that you understand and are there for them by paying close attention, keeping eye contact, and expressing empathy.
- Openness and Honesty: Promote an environment where people are honest and transparent by discussing your needs, wants, and worries with your spouse in a courteous and nonjudgmental way.
- Vulnerability: Being open and honest about your worries, anxieties, and deeper feelings with your spouse fosters emotional connection and trust.
- Empathy: Despite your disagreement, strive to comprehend your partner's point of view by acknowledging their experiences, viewpoints, and feelings.
- Conflict Resolution: By approaching disagreements constructively, hearing each other out, looking for areas of agreement, and pursuing mutually agreeable solutions, you can develop healthy conflict resolution abilities.

Emotional Connection: - Quality Time: Make the most of your time together by doing important things, talking about things you both have in common, and sharing experiences that deepen your emotional connection.
- Express Affection: Express affection with words of love and gratitude as well as physical touch, embraces, kisses, and cuddles.
- Show Your Gratitude: Showing gratitude to your partner for their actions, contributions, and attributes improves your relationship and fosters happy emotions.
- Emotional Support: Be there for someone emotionally when they need it, listen to them sympathetically, and offer consolation, encouragement, and affirmation.

3. Physical Intimacy: - Intimate Touch: Physical contact, such holding hands, giving hugs, and giving soft strokes, promotes emotional intimacy and fondness.

- Prioritize sexual closeness by keeping a happy and healthy sexual life, talking to your partner about your preferences and desires, and experimenting with new techniques to increase intimacy and pleasure.

- Non-Sexual contact: Using non-sexual contact in your regular encounters, including snuggling, massages, and back rubs, can strengthen your bonds and foster a sense of connection.

4. Intellectual Intimacy: - Have Meaningful Conversations: Bring up subjects of shared interest, exchange viewpoints, ideas, and personal experiences, and have in-depth discussions that pique curiosity and intellectual connection.

Encourage one another's intellectual interests, pastimes, and personal growth. Share in milestone celebrations and accomplishments. - Support Intellectual Growth.

5. Shared Activities and Rituals: - Establish Shared Rituals: Make traditions or rituals that are important to you both. These can be date evenings, weekly meals, movie nights, or morning routines that help to fortify your relationship and make enduring memories.

- Explore New Experiences: Take up new pursuits, excursions, or pastimes as a pair to foster excitement, shared experiences, and chances for development.

6. Creating Security and Trust: - Be Trustworthy Show consistency, dependability, and dependability in both your words and deeds to foster a relationship based on trust and security.

"- Recognize your boundaries: Respect each other's personal space, independence, privacy, and individuality. Be honest with one another about your preferences and boundaries.

7. Develop Emotional Intimacy: - Discuss Dreams and Goals: As a couple or as an individual, talk about your long-term objectives and dreams, and cooperate to help each other reach your goals.

- Celebrate Successes: Honor each other's victories, landmarks, and accomplishments. Also, recognize the advantages and contributions that each partner offers the partnership.
- Practice Forgiveness: Recognize your faults, provide an apology when required, and resolve conflicts with empathy and compassion in order to foster a culture of understanding, forgiveness, and acceptance.

Spiritual intimacy can be achieved by exploring shared ideas, values, practices, and rituals that strengthen the spiritual bond and feeling of purpose between couples, provided that spirituality is a priority for both.
- Encourage Each Other's Spiritual Journey: Participate in meaningful conversations on spiritual issues that are important to you both, and encourage each other's spiritual development, exploration, and practices.

Self-Awareness: Examine your own needs, feelings, triggers, and communication preferences. Be open to learning from experiences and criticism. This leads to self-reflection and growth.
- Personal Development: Take part in activities that promote your well-being, sense of self-worth, and capacity to make a constructive contribution to the relationship.
- Couples Therapy: If you want to develop your relationship and intimacy as a pair, address any underlying issues, and improve communication, think about getting couples therapy or counseling.

You may build a solid and satisfying relationship with your partner by implementing these techniques and tactics into your partnership. You can also increase intimacy and emotional connection.

Sexual Satisfaction and Quality Relationship:

These two dimensions of romantic relationships are closely related and play a major role in both general wellbeing and emotional and relational fulfillment. Taking into account a variety of aspects that affect closeness, communication, mutual pleasure, and emotional connection within the relationship is necessary to comprehend the interplay between sexual satisfaction and relationship quality. The impact of sexual satisfaction on the quality of relationships is examined in detail below:

1. Determining What Sexual Contentment Is:

- The subjective sense of pleasure, fulfillment, and contentment that a person feels from their sexual life and interactions is referred to as sexual satisfaction. The relationship's sexual compatibility, intimacy, emotional connection, physical pleasure, and communication are all included.

The following elements influence sexual satisfaction: arousal, orgasmic experiences, sexual communication, experimenting, fantasy exploration, emotional closeness, and general relationship dynamics.

2. Quality of relationships:

- Positive elements of the romantic connection, overall well-being, and satisfaction are referred to as relationship quality. Relationship happiness is a result of a combination of factors such as emotional connection, communication, trust, intimacy, commitment, mutual support, and shared goals.

Emotions of intimacy, comprehension, respect, gratitude, support, and stability in the connection are characteristics of high-quality relationships.

The connection between quality relationship and sexual satisfaction:

- Improved Emotional Intimacy: A relationship's emotional intimacy, connection, and trust are all improved by sexual fulfillment. Stronger bonds between partners are created through fulfilling sexual encounters, honest discussion of preferences and wishes, and reciprocal sexual enjoyment.

- Communication and Understanding: Direct and honest communication between partners about their needs, desires, and worries about sex promotes empathy, understanding, and responsiveness, which improves both the quality of the relationship and the level of sexual satisfaction.

- Mutual Fulfillment: Responding to one another's needs and desires as well as having mutual sexual satisfaction foster a sense of reciprocity and relationship contentment.

The relationship happiness of a couple is positively correlated with their level of sexual pleasure because closeness, emotional connection, and overall well-being are frequently linked to sexual fulfillment.

- Resolving Conflicts: Pleasure and happy sexual encounters can act as buffers between partners in a relationship, assisting them in navigating tensions, obstacles, and arguments more skillfully.

The following factors affect the quality of relationships and sexual satisfaction:

- Effective conversation: Relationship harmony and sexual satisfaction are fostered by open and honest conversation regarding sexual preferences, boundaries, desires, and concerns.

- Emotional Connection: Deeper feelings of understanding and connection between partners are fostered by emotional intimacy, trust, vulnerability, and empathy. These factors also add to sexual satisfaction and the quality of relationships.

- Compatible: Relationship compatibility and sexual satisfaction within a partnership are influenced by shared sexual ideals, attitudes, and interests as well as sexual compatibility.

The quality of a relationship and sexual satisfaction can be influenced by a person's physical and mental well-being, mental and sexual health, stress management, and general sense of well-being.

- Relationship Dynamics: A couple's communication style, power dynamics, unresolved issues, and disputes all have an impact on the quality of their relationship, including sexual satisfaction.

The dynamics of relationships can be affected by life transitions including motherhood, job changes, and aging, which calls for cooperation, communication, and flexibility in order to maintain sexual satisfaction.

Ways to Improve Quality Relationship and Sexual Satisfaction:

Establish a secure and transparent atmosphere for talking to your spouse about your needs, wants, and dreams related to sex, and be open to their suggestions and preferences.

- Mutual Exploration: To increase arousal, pleasure, and novelty in the relationship, both partners should explore novel sexual experiences, tasks, fantasies, and approaches.

Prioritize Intimacy: To promote intimacy and closeness outside of sexual encounters, give priority to quality time, love, non-sexual touch, and emotional intimacy.

obstacles: Through open conversation, empathy, and, if necessary, professional assistance, address any obstacles or issues pertaining to sexual health, performance anxiety, body image issues, past traumas, or relationship conflicts.

- Regular Check-Ins: See your spouse on a regular basis to talk about goals, satisfaction levels, and areas for growth. You may also work together to improve the quality of your relationship and your sexual fulfillment.

To address any sexual difficulties, enhance communication, and fortify intimacy and relationship happiness, think about enlisting the help of a licensed therapist or counselor who specializes in couples therapy or sex therapy.

In conclusion, there is a strong correlation between the quality of a romantic relationship and its sexual satisfaction. Emotional closeness, connection, and general well-being are all improved by having fulfilling sexual encounters and having open communication. Maximizing emotional closeness, mutual understanding, and fulfillment can result in a satisfying, healthy relationship dynamic and increased sexual satisfaction.

CHAPTER SIX

Sexual Expression and Behavior:

A vast array of behaviors, attitudes, convictions, and experiences pertaining to intimacy and sexuality are included in the category of sexual behavior and expression. Individual variances, cultural conventions, societal views, personal ideals, and interpersonal dynamics all have an impact on these elements. Examining a range of factors, such as sexual orientation, identity, interests, attitudes, consent, and communication, is necessary to comprehend sexual behavior and expression. This is a thorough examination of sexual expression and behavior:

1. Identity and Sexual Orientation:

- Sexual Orientation: A person's emotional, romantic, and sexual inclinations toward other people are referred to as their sexual orientation. The following are common sexual orientations: asexual (absence of sexual attraction), bisexual (attraction to both genders), heterosexual (attraction to the opposite gender), and homosexual (attraction to the same gender).

- Gender Identity: A person's internal perception of their gender may or may not correspond with the sex they were assigned at birth. Sexual orientation and the ways in which people exhibit their sexuality can be influenced by gender identity.

2. Sexual Fantasies and Preferences:

- Sexual Preferences: These are the particular traits, actions, or activities that people find stimulating or sexually appealing. Individual preferences might differ greatly and encompass a wide range of pursuits, occupations, fetishes, and role-playing situations.

- Sexual Fantasies: Imaginary or mental images of sexual pleasure, arousal, and desire are known as sexual fantasies. Fantasies play a part in sexual arousal and fulfillment and might be based on personal experiences, wants, taboos, or made-up scenarios.

3. Perceptions and Opinions Regarding Sexuality:

- Cultural and Religious Influences: Attitudes toward modesty, sexual roles, acceptable sexual practices, and sexuality are influenced by cultural and religious norms, values, and beliefs.

- Sexual Education: People's views, knowledge, and behaviors regarding sexuality are shaped by both formal and informal sexual education, which includes knowledge about anatomy, reproduction, contraception, consent, pleasure, and sexual health.

- Media and Society: Perceptions, expectations, and actions pertaining to sexuality and sexual expression can be influenced by media depictions, social media, pornography, and cultural messages about beauty, sexuality, gender roles, and relationships.

4. Communication and Consent:

- Consent: The voluntary, mutual decision to participate in sexual activity is referred to as consent. Clear, passionate, continuous, and freely provided consent that is free from compulsion, manipulation, or pressure is required.

- Communication: Respectful relationships, positive sexual experiences, and mutual fulfillment all depend on effective communication regarding sexual desires, boundaries, preferences, and expectations. Between sexual partners, open communication fosters understanding, consent, and response.

5. Sexual Wellness and Health:

- Sexual Health: All aspects of well-being associated to sexuality, including mental, emotional, physical, and social, are included in sexual health. It covers topics like sexual function, enjoyment, safety, contraception, STI prevention, and sexual consent in addition to reproductive health.

- Sexual Well-Being: Having satisfactory, agreeable, and good sexual encounters enhances one's sense of general wellbeing, self-worth, and contentment in relationships.

6. Investigating and Testing:

- Sexual Exploration: Through self-examination, conversation with partners, and attempting novel behaviors or experiences, people can engage in sexual exploration to learn about their preferences, boundaries, and wants.

- Sexual Experimentation: Within consensual and courteous bounds, sexual experimentation is investigating novel methods, fantasies, role-playing, toys, or activities to augment sexual pleasure, intimacy, and fulfillment.

7. Difficulties and Things to Remember:

- Sexual Dysfunction: Issues with sexual behavior and expression, such as erectile dysfunction, early ejaculation, low desire, or pain during sexual activity, may necessitate medical or therapeutic interventions.

- Sexual Identity and Acceptance: People may have difficulties with regard to their sexual orientation, acceptance of who they are, coming out, stigma from society, prejudice, and acceptance in their social and cultural environments.

- Relationship Dynamics: Communication styles, power dynamics, emotional ties, and partner compatibility all have an impact on sexual behavior and expression.

8. Self-expression and Empowerment:

- Sexual Empowerment: Promoting positive attitudes about sexual expression, enjoyment, and diversity as well as embracing one's own sexuality, desires, and preferences are all part of sexual empowerment.

- Self-Expression: Respecting the autonomy, rights, and boundaries of others while expressing one's own sexuality, wants, boundaries, and identity in a genuine and self-assured manner is referred to as sexual self-expression.

In conclusion, sexual expression and behavior are intricate and varied facets of human sexuality that are impacted by relationship dynamics, cultural conventions, society views, individual characteristics, and personal ideals. Within a variety of social and cultural situations, sexual health, well-being, happiness, and empowerment are enhanced by an understanding of and commitment to healthy, consensual, and respectful sexual conduct and expression.

Variations in Sexual Behavior:

These encompass the wide diversity of actions, inclinations, orientations, and practices that people can choose as a means of expressing their sexuality. Interpersonal dynamics, cultural norms, societal attitudes, biological factors, psychological factors, and personal beliefs all have an impact on these variances. The following are some typical sexual behavior variations:

1. Sexual Orientation: - Heterosexuality: This describes relationships (such as those between men and women) and sexual attraction and desire between people of different genders.
- Homosexuality: This refers to relationships (such as those between men and women or between men and boys) and sexual attraction and desire among people of the same gender.
- Bisexuality: This refers to sexual attraction, desire, and relationships with people of both genders without being exclusively drawn to one.
- Pansexuality: Relationships and sexual attraction based on romantic, emotional, or sexual attraction to someone regardless of gender identity or biological sex are referred to as pansexual.

2. Expression and Identity of Gender: - Cisgender: People who identify as cisgender identify with the gender that was given to them at birth, and their gender identity corresponds with their biological sex.
Transgender: People who identify as transgender have a gender identification that is different from the sex they were assigned at birth. Pronouns, attire, looks, and social duties are some ways that transgender people show their gender identification.
- Non-Binary and Genderqueer: People who identify as non-binary or genderqueer go beyond the conventional dichotomy of male and female genders. Their gender identities could be ambiguous, or they might exhibit traits that are non-binary, masculine, or feminine.

3. Sexual Preferences and Practices: - Monogamy: This refers to the practice of people having emotional and sexual exclusivity with one partner at a time throughout a relationship.

- Non-Monogamy: There are other types of non-monogamy, including swinging, open relationships, polyamory (consensual partnerships with numerous people), and other morally-responsible non-monogamy.

- Casual Sex: Often involving one-time encounters or brief sexual relationships, casual sex is defined as sexual actions carried out without a committed or romantic connection.

The terms "kink" and "BDSM" (Bondage, Discipline, Dominance, Submission, Sadism, and Masochism) refer to a social construct that includes role-playing, consensual sexual activities, power dynamics, and the investigation of fetishes and fantasies.

- Fetishes: These are strong fancies, interests, or passions in sexual matters that center upon certain items, body parts, actions, or circumstances that heighten arousal.

- Sexual Health Practices: These include communicating about sexual health and limits, using condoms and getting regular STI testing; they also involve safer sexual behaviors such as contraception and education on sexual health.

4. Interpersonal Conduct in Sexual Life:
Teenage years: During this time, people experiment with their sexual identities, desires, and relationships. They also frequently see changes in their levels of sexual arousal, attraction, and conduct.

- Young Adulthood: Young adults are sexually exploratory, date, and create close relationships. They have varying sexual experiences, interests, and behaviors.

- Midlife and Later Years: Physical health, hormonal changes, relationship dynamics, and life transitions are some of the factors that can influence how a person behaves sexually in these years.

Cultural norms, values, traditions, and religious beliefs determine attitudes about sexuality, sexual expression, gender roles, relationships, and sexual activities. These are the five cultural and societal influences.

- Social views: People's choices about how to display their sexuality, get sexual health care, and negotiate relationships with others are influenced by societal views, stigma, discrimination, and legislative frameworks.

Psychological and emotional factors that affect sexual desire include libido variations, frequency of sexual activity, arousal levels, and receptivity to sexual stimuli.
- Sexual Satisfaction: Depending on elements like sexual compatibility, communication, emotional closeness, and the satisfaction of one's own wants and desires, a person's level of sexual satisfaction may vary.
- Self-Esteem and Body Image: These factors can affect sexual habits, comfort level during sexual activities, and enjoyment of sex. They can also affect one's confidence, self-esteem, and body image.

7. Interpersonal Dynamics: -Talking openly and honestly about preferences, boundaries, consent, and sexual wants is crucial for negotiating sexual behavior differences and guaranteeing respect and satisfaction for both parties.
Relationship dynamics, emotional connection, trust, communication methods, and closeness levels between partners can all influence sexual behavior variations.
- Negotiation of Needs: In a partnership, partners use mutual respect, discussion, and compromise to work through differences in sexual preferences, expectations, and boundaries.

To sum up, sexual behavior variations cover a wide range of expressions, orientations, practices, and preferences that are impacted by biological, cultural, psychological, and interpersonal parameters. Promoting sexual health, diversity, consent, and empowerment among varied individuals and groups is made possible by acknowledging and accepting these variances.

Sexual Fantasies and Preoccupations:

Aspects of human sexuality that entail creative ideas, cravings, or preferences for particular actions, things, situations, or behaviors that heighten sexual arousal, pleasure, or gratification are known as sexual fantasies and fetishes. Individual preferences, psychological variables, cultural influences, and life experiences can all have an impact on these fetishes and fantasies, which differ greatly throughout people. An extensive examination of sexual obsessions and fantasies may be found here:

1. Sexual Fantasies: - Definition: Conceivable or mental ideas, thoughts, or scenarios that arouse, excite, or please the sex are known as sexual fantasies. They can contain a variety of themes, from private and romantic moments to obscene or unusual thoughts.
- Common topics: Typical topics for sexual fantasies include romantic relationships, daring adventures, power struggles, taboo or forbidden situations, role-playing, dominance/submission, voyeurism, exhibitionism, group sex, or certain body parts or characteristics.
An Individual's ability to explore desires, fantasies, and scenarios that might not be realistic or suitable in real-life situations makes sexual fantasies a significant factor in sexual arousal, stimulation, and fulfillment.

2. Sexual Fetishes: - Definition: Sexual fetishes are defined as strong sexual interests, cravings, or arousal linked to particular things, body parts, substances, activities, or situations that aren't often thought of as sexually stimulating by others.
- Types of Fetishes: Common fetish types include the following: role-playing fetishes (e.g., nurse-patient, teacher-student), latex or leather fetishes, body part fetishes (e.g., breasts, buttocks), BDSM (Bondage, Discipline, Dominance, Submission, Sadism, and Masochism) practices, lingerie or clothing fetishes, and body part fetishes (e.g., buttocks, breasts, buttocks).
Origin and Development: A range of factors, including as early life experiences, exposure to certain stimuli, conditioning, cultural influences, psychological

associations, and individual preferences, can contribute to the development of fetishes. Not every fetish has a distinct or obvious beginning.

- Function in Sexual Expression: Those who possess fetishes may use them in their fantasies, sexual acts, or relationships with partners who consent, all of which can increase their level of arousal, excitement, and fulfillment.

3. Examining Sensual Fantasies and Fetishes: - Consent and Communication: It's critical to investigate sexual fantasies and fetishes in a polite and consensual setting. Ensuring that activities are pleasurable and agreeable for both partners requires open communication about boundaries, comfort zones, and wants.

- Fantasy versus Reality: It's critical to distinguish between sexual fantasies (conceived ideas or situations) and actual actions. Although fantasies might heighten feelings of arousal and pleasure, they do not always correspond with behaviors or preferences in the real world.

- Acceptance and Understanding: People who have fetishes or sexual fantasies should make an effort to accept and understand their cravings without feeling guilty or condemned. Realizing that sexual diversity and variation are typical facets of human sexuality is crucial.

Seeking Help: People can seek help from mental health specialists, sex therapists, or counselors who specialize in sexual health and well-being if their sexual fantasies or fetishes cause them distress, impairment, or relationship problems.

4. Cultural and Social Considerations: - Cultural Attitudes: There are significant cultural differences in attitudes, fetishes, and sexual expression norms among countries and cultures. Certain sexual desires or fetishes may be natural or acceptable in some cultures, while stigmatized or pathologize others.

- Legal and Ethical Issues: It's critical to understand the legal and ethical issues surrounding sexual behavior, consent, privacy, and respecting the limits and autonomy of others. Fetish-related activities need to be lawful and always consenting.

5. Healthful Sexual Expression and Exploration: - Self-Exploration: Through introspection, fantasy exploration, and self-examination, people can safely and discreetly explore their sexual fantasies, desires, and preferences.

Enhancing Intimacy, Mutual Understanding, and Sexual Satisfaction in Relationships: Partners can communicate about their sexual fantasies, desires, and boundaries in an open and nonjudgmental manner.

Consensual Play: For individuals and couples with similar interests and boundaries, engaging in consensual role-playing, fantasy exploration, and incorporating fetishes into sexual activities can be gratifying and pleasurable experiences.

To sum up, sexual fantasies and fetishes are unique and varied facets of human sexuality that can improve a person's level of sexual arousal, pleasure, and satisfaction. To explore sexual desires and fetishes in a respectful, healthy, and consensual way, understanding, acceptance, communication, and consent are essential components.

Social and Cultural Influences on Sexual Expression:

In a variety of cultures and communities, social and cultural factors have a big impact on how people behave and how they think about sexual expression. The way that people view, experience, and express their sexuality is influenced by a variety of factors, including gender roles, family relationships, religious teachings, media depictions, cultural norms, and legal frameworks. An examination of the impact of culture and society on sexual expression is provided below:

1. Norms and Cultural Values:

Cultural diversity refers to the attitudes, beliefs, and norms that differ among cultures in relation to intimacy, modesty, sexuality, and sexual expression. People's views, actions, and experiences with sex and relationships are influenced by these cultural variances.

- Cultural Taboos: There may be taboos or limits in some cultures regarding having sex, exploring one's sexual impulses, or having sex outside of certain settings, such as marriage or childbearing.

- Sexual Double Standards: Certain cultures may have differing expectations and standards for men and women with relation to sexual expression, promiscuity, modesty, and sexual freedom.

2. Religious Doctrine and Beliefs: - Religious Influence: Within religious groups, religious doctrines, beliefs, and teachings frequently impact attitudes and behaviors regarding marriage, sexual ethics, sexuality, contraception, abortion, LGBTQ+ rights, and gender roles.

Morality and Sin: Sexual expression is subject to cultural taboos, stigma, and prohibitions because certain religious traditions consider particular sexual actions or expressions to be sinful, immoral, or forbidden.

3. Expectations from Society and Gender Roles:

- Gender Expectations: Depending on cultural standards of masculinity, femininity, sexual assertiveness, and sexual agency, gender roles and societal expectations can influence how people express their sexuality.

- Socialization: People are conditioned to conform to particular gender norms and expectations concerning modesty, sexual desire, initiating sexual activity, and sexual behavior.

Social Scripts: Sexual initiation, marriage, romantic partnerships, and courting are all subjects of cultural scripts and narratives that shape how people view and engage in sexual expression in social settings.

The fourth area of discussion is media representations and influences. The media, which includes advertising, movies, television, and internet platforms, shapes cultural standards, conventions, and perceptions of beauty, sexuality, relationships, and sexual conduct.

- Sexualization: Society's ideals of beauty and sexualized imagery shape people's perceptions of appearance, desirability, and sexual expression. The media frequently sexualizes bodies, relationships, and behaviors.

The fifth factor to consider is the influence of family dynamics and upbringing on an individual's views, beliefs, and values regarding intimacy, consent, sexuality, and sexual expression.

Parental Influence: By communicating with them, modeling behavior, and passing down cultural beliefs, parents and other caregivers have an impact on their children's conceptions of sex, relationships, gender roles, limits, and sexual ideals.

6. Frameworks for Law and Policy:

The legal regulations pertaining to sexual health, reproductive rights, LGBTQ+ rights, consent, sexual harassment, and sex education have an impact on the freedoms and rights of individuals to express themselves sexually in society.

- Sex Education: There are cultural differences in the availability and content of sex education programs, curriculum, and resources, which can have an impact on people's knowledge, attitudes, and actions about relationships, consent, and sexual health.

7. Social Movements and Advocacy: - Sexual Rights: Pushing back against stigma, prejudice, and oppression associated with sexuality, social movements, advocacy

groups, and human rights initiatives support sexual rights, autonomy, consent, and freedom of sexual expression.

LGBTQ+ rights movements seek to promote equality, acceptance, and visibility for people with a range of sexual orientations, gender identities, and expressions. They also aim to challenge cultural and societal conventions that limit sexual diversity and inclusion.

8. cross-cultural variants: - Cultural diversity: how various societies and communities view and govern marriage, relationships, sexual expression, gender roles, and sexual health are examples of cross-cultural variations.

- Globalization: Migration, globalization, and cultural exchanges all contribute to the exchange of various cultural viewpoints, behaviors, and attitudes around sexuality, which raises knowledge of, and tolerance for, the diversity of sexual expression.

In summary, people's views, beliefs, values, and behaviors around intimacy, relationships, sexual expression, and sexual rights are shaped by cultural and societal factors in a variety of nations and communities. In conversations about sexuality, consent, diversity, and sexual health across cultures and situations, an awareness of these impacts promotes inclusivity, empowerment, respect, and awareness.

Handling Problems with Sexual Functions:

Physical, psychological, relational, and contextual aspects that impact sexual health and well-being are all addressed in a comprehensive approach to managing sexual disorders and dysfunctions. Depending on the needs and circumstances of each patient, various interventions, therapies, and techniques may be needed to address various sexual difficulties and dysfunctions. Managing sexual problems and dysfunctions involves the following crucial elements:

1. Recognizing the Problem: - Determine the Issue Clearly define and comprehend the particular sexual problem or malfunction, such as low libido, erectile dysfunction, dyspareunia (pain during intercourse), problems with arousal or orgasm, or low libido.
Investigate Causes: Examine the following: physical health concerns, hormone imbalances, drugs, psychological variables (such as stress, anxiety, or depression), relationship problems, traumatic experiences in the past, and environmental influences are examples of possible causes and contributing factors.

2. Medical Evaluation and Therapy: - Speak with a Healthcare Provider: Consult a qualified healthcare provider for assessment and advice, such as a gynecologist, endocrinologist, urologist, or sexual health specialist, in order to identify and treat any underlying medical issues or physical factors that may be contributing to the sexual difficulty.
- Medication and Therapies: To address the sexual issue, medical treatments, medications (e.g., hormone therapy, erectile dysfunction meds), or interventions (e.g., pelvic floor therapy for sexual pain) may be suggested based on the diagnosis.

3. Psychological Support and Therapy: - Try counseling or sex therapy with a certified therapist or a sex therapist who focuses on relationships and sexual health. In addition to body image concerns and sexual fears, sex therapy can help address psychological variables, relationship dynamics, communication problems, and past traumas that may have an affect on sexual functioning.

- Cognitive-Behavioral Therapy (CBT): CBT methods can help with self-esteem problems, performing anxiety, negative thought patterns, and behavioral adjustments linked to sexual functioning.
- Relaxation and Mindfulness: Techniques like progressive muscle relaxation, deep breathing, mindfulness, and meditation can help lessen tension, stress, and anxiety—all of which can exacerbate sexual problems.

Lifestyle Modifications: - Adopt a healthy lifestyle to support general well-being and sexual health. This includes regular exercise, a balanced diet, enough sleep, stress management strategies, and abstaining from drug abuse (such as excessive alcohol or tobacco use).
- Handling Hormonal Imbalances: Engage with medical professionals to investigate hormone replacement therapy or other suitable therapies for conditions relating to hormonal imbalances (such as low testosterone, menopause-related hormonal changes).

5. Communication and Relationship Enhancement: - Encourage Honest and Open Communication: Talk to your spouse about your needs, wants, boundaries, and expectations regarding sex. Good communication fosters empathy, cooperation, understanding, and support amongst partners in the management of sexual concerns.
- Relationship counseling: To handle problems in your relationship, work on your communication abilities, get closer, and handle sexual matters in the framework of your partnership, think about couples therapy or relationship counseling.

6. Educational and Self-Help Materials: - Sexual Education: Provide your partner and yourself with information on sexual anatomy, consent, pleasure, sexual response cycles, and common sexual health concerns. It is possible to lessen stigma, fear, and false beliefs about sexuality by being aware of these factors.
- Self-Help Materials: Examine books, online discussion boards, self-help tools, and instructional materials on intimacy, sexual function, sexual health, and relationship building. Peer help and insightful discussions can also be obtained by taking part in support groups or online communities.

7. Consulting Experts and Specialists:
- Specialist Referrals: Seek advice from specialists such as sex therapists, sexual medicine specialists, psychologists, psychiatrists, or experts in reproductive health for a thorough assessment, diagnosis, and treatment planning, depending on the particular sexual issue or dysfunction.
- Alternative Therapies: Some treatments for sexual difficulties may benefit from the addition of alternative therapies including acupuncture, mindfulness-based exercises, herbal supplements, or holistic methods. Consult medical professionals about these choices before to attempting them.

8. Frequent Inspection and Tracking:
- Follow-Up Care: Make sure you schedule routine follow-up visits with your healthcare providers to assess any new issues, track your progress, and receive complete care for your sexual health and well-being.
- Monitor Progress: To inform continued care and assistance, chart any alterations, advancements, or difficulties pertaining to sexual functioning, emotional health, and relationship dynamics.

Keep in mind that treating sexual problems and dysfunctions frequently calls for a customized, multifaceted strategy that takes into account environmental, relational, psychological, and physical aspects. Seeking professional advice, having honest conversations with your spouse, and investigating methods and remedies that support sexual health, fulfillment, and general wellbeing are all crucial.

CHAPTER SEVEN

Gender and Sexuality:

These are two intricately linked facets of the human experience and identity. Gender and sexuality definitions, variations, intersections, social constructions, and implications within a range of cultural, social, and personal settings must all be explored in order to fully comprehend these ideas. This is a thorough examination of gender and sexuality:

1. Identification of Gender:

Gender identity is defined as an individual's firmly held perception of their own gender, which may or may not correspond with the sex to which they were biologically assigned at birth. A person's perception of being male, female, both, neither, or a combination of genders is included in their gender identity, which is an internal and subjective experience of self.

- Gender Diversity: People can identify as cisgender (behaving in accordance with the sex they were assigned at birth), transgender (identifying with a gender other than their assigned sex), non-binary (identifying as something other than the traditional binary of male and female), genderqueer, genderfluid, agender, or as other gender identities.

2. Personality:

A person's sexual orientation, as well as their wants, attractions, fantasies, behaviors, and relationships, are referred to as their sexuality. It includes the passionate, sensual, and emotional facets of the human experience and varies greatly from person to person.

- Sexual Orientation: The pattern of an individual's romantic, emotional, and sexual attraction to others is referred to as their sexual orientation. Typical sexual orientations include asexual (not attracted to any gender), bisexual (attraction to both genders), heterosexual (attraction to the same gender), homosexual (attraction to the opposite gender), and other orientations along the spectrum of attraction.

- Flexibility and Exploration: Sexuality is dynamic and open to exploration, self-discovery, and long-term shifts. Throughout their lives, people may go through phases of changing interests, desires, or identities.

3. The points where gender and sexuality intersect:

- Sexual orientation and gender identity: Although these two components of identification are separate, they can interact and have an impact on one another. A transgender person's gender identity, for instance, may have an impact on how they perceive their sexual orientation and attraction.

Gender Expression and Sexual Attraction: Gender expression encompasses how people show themselves externally (clothes, looks, mannerisms, etc.) and can have an impact on how people express their sexuality, find partners, and manage relationships.

4. Cultural and Social Constructions:

- Socially Constructed Nature: Cultural norms, ideas, values, stereotypes, expectations, and power dynamics within cultures determine the social construction of gender and sexuality. These structures affect people's perceptions, experiences, and expressions of gender and sexuality.

Cultural Divergences: Personal experiences with gender and sexuality are influenced by societal and cultural perspectives on gender roles, sexual behaviors, identities, and relationships, which differ greatly between cultures and historical periods.

5. Expectations and Roles for Gender:

Traditional gender roles: Based on given sex, many civilizations have gender norms and expectations that dictate specific behaviors, tasks, obligations, and expressions (e.g., masculinity for males, femininity for females). These roles can affect how people manage their gender identification, expression, and interpersonal interactions.

- Gender Stereotypes: Stereotypes refer to inflexible or simplistic ideas about the qualities, roles, and behaviors that are associated with certain genders. Promoting gender equality and diversity requires dismantling and challenging preconceptions.

6. Advocacy for Sexual Rights:

The rights to autonomy, privacy, consent, information, non-discrimination, access to sexual health care, and freedom from violence, coercion, and discrimination on the basis of sexual orientation or gender identity are all included in the category of sexual rights.

-LGBTQ+ Advocacy: By promoting visibility, acceptance, equality, and human rights for people with varied gender identities and sexual orientations, LGBTQ+ (Lesbian, Gay, Bisexual, Transgender, Queer/Questioning, and Others) advocacy movements challenge stigma, prejudice, and social barriers.

7. Expression of Self:

- Self-identification: A person's gender identification and sexual orientation are essential components of who they are, and they can have an impact on how they manage relationships, social interactions, communities, and personal development.

- Gender Expression: Gender expression is the external ways in which people show their gender identification through language, behaviors, appearance, grooming, and social roles. Diverse gender expressions don't necessarily conform to stereotypes or cultural norms.

8. Well-being and Sexual Health:

Encouraging awareness, respect, consent, diversity, and well-informed decision-making around sexuality, gender, relationships, sexual health, and reproductive rights are the goals of comprehensive sexual education.

- Sexual Health Services: It is crucial to provide everyone with access to comprehensive sexual health services, such as counseling, support, STI testing and treatment, reproductive healthcare, and contraception, in order to promote sexual health, well-being, and empowerment.

In summary, biological, social, cultural, and psychological variables all have an impact on gender and sexuality, which are complex facets of human identity and experience. Promoting inclusivity, equality, autonomy, and well-being among diverse persons and groups requires an understanding of and respect for a range of gender identities, sexual orientations, expressions, and experiences.

Gender Identity and Sexual Orientation:

Although they are two different facets of the human experience, they are linked together. In order to foster inclusion, acceptance, and understanding across varied cultures, it is crucial to comprehend the distinctions and links between these ideas. This is where we will get more into each of these ideas:

1. Identification of Gender:

- Definition: Gender identity is the deeply held belief about one's own gender, which may or may not correspond with the sex that was biologically given to one at birth. It is an inward, intimate experience of who one is; it includes feelings of being either male or female, neither, both, or of a different gender entirely.

- Diversity of Gender Identities: Gender identity is not limited to the conventional male/female binary. Gender identities on the spectrum include non-binary, genderqueer, genderfluid, agender, bigender, and transgender. Cisgender people identify as such, while transgender people identify as different from their assigned sex.

- Presentation and Expression: Gender identification affects how people present themselves externally through language, behaviors, attire, grooming, and social roles. It's possible for gender expression to be flexible, diverse, and nonconforming to stereotypes or societal norms.

- Respect and Acceptance: Determining a person's gender identity and confirming it through the use of their preferred names, pronouns, and identities upholds their autonomy, dignity, and inclusivity.

2. In terms of sexual orientation:

- Definition: An individual's pattern of romantic, emotional, and sexual attraction to others is referred to as their sexual orientation. It includes the identities and gender-based experiences of attraction and desire.

- Typical Sexual Orientations: Typical sexual orientations consist of:

Attraction to people of the opposite gender is known as heterosexuality.

Attraction to people of the same gender is a sign of homosexuality.

Attraction to people of both genders is known as bisexuality.

Attraction to people irrespective of their gender identity is known as pansexuality.

Asexuality: The absence of sexual attraction or a negligible desire to engage in sexual behavior.

- Fluidity and Complexity: Individuals' sexual orientations can be dynamic, varied, and fluid over time, resulting in changes, explorations, and variances in their attractions and desires.

Respecting variety: It is important to foster inclusivity, equality, and respect for sexual variety by accepting and validating the multiplicity of identities and attractions as well as individuals' sexual orientations.

3. Connections and Intersections:

- How Gender Identity and Sexual Orientation Interact: While there are connections between gender identity and sexual orientation, they are not the same thing. For instance:

- A woman who identifies as cisgender may be heterosexual, bisexual, lesbian, or have another sexual orientation. Heterosexuals are drawn to males. Bisexuals are drawn to women.

A transgender man's desire to women can lead him to identify as heterosexual, as gay, as bisexual, or as some other sexual orientation.

- Based on their attraction to people of different genders, non-binary, genderqueer, or genderfluid people may have a variety of sexual orientations.

- Intersectionality: This is the term used to describe how several facets of identity, including gender identity, sexual orientation, race, ethnicity, culture, socioeconomic status, disability, and other variables, overlap and are connected to one another. awareness people's experiences, viewpoints, and difficulties in a variety of circumstances requires an awareness of intersectionality.

4. Obstacles and Lobbying:

- Stigma and Discrimination: People may experience stigma, marginalization, discrimination, and difficulties because of their sexual orientation, gender identity, or the intersection of these identities. This may affect one's well-being, social acceptance, mental health, and access to resources.

- Advocacy and Support: These days, acceptance, equality, rights, and visibility for people of all gender identities and sexual orientations are greatly enhanced by advocacy campaigns, LGBTQ+ rights movements, education, awareness campaigns, and supportive communities.

- Legal Protections: In order to guarantee people's rights, safety, and well-being regardless of their gender identity or sexual orientation, supportive surroundings, anti-discrimination laws, and inclusive healthcare practices are crucial.

The diversity, identity, and self-expression of humans are inextricably linked to gender identity and sexual orientation. Fostering inclusivity, respect, dignity, and support for people of varied gender identities and sexual orientations within society requires an understanding of the distinctions, intersections, and complexity of these ideas.

Transgender and Non-Binary Experiences:

Encompassing a variety of identities, expressions, struggles, and affirmations within the larger context of gender variation, transgender and non-binary experiences are described. The diversity, complexity, and individual journeys of people who identify as transgender or non-binary must be acknowledged in order to fully comprehend these experiences. Let's investigate these ideas further:

1. transgender experiences: - Transgender is a term used to describe people whose gender identity is different from the sex they were assigned at birth. It is frequently shortened to "trans." When it comes to social, medical, and legal transitions to conform to their gender identification, transgender people might identify as binary (male or female) or non-binary.
- Gender Dysphoria: The discomfort or anguish brought on by the mismatch between one's ascribed sex and gender identity is a condition that many transgender people report having. Gender dysphoria can be lessened for many people by gender-affirming procedures such hormone therapy, surgery, or social transition.
- Adopting a name, pronouns, outfit, appearance, and social roles that correspond with one's gender identity is known as social transition. Prior to or concurrent with a medical transition, it is a crucial part of reaffirming one's gender identity.
- Medical Transition: Medication to match secondary sex traits to a person's gender identity, such as hormone replacement treatment (HRT), and surgical operations like genital (bottom) or chest (top) surgery are examples of medical transition. Individual decisions regarding medical transition are made by transgender people, and not all of them pursue it.
- Legal Recognition: Protecting transgender people from discrimination based on their gender identity and granting them legal rights to change their names, gender markers on identification documents, and other benefits are essential to securing their identities and rights.

2. Non-Binary Experiences: - The term "non-binary" (also known as "enby") refers to those whose gender identity does not fall neatly into the male or female binary. The gender identities of non-binary people can be completely distinct from conventional notions of gender, a combination of male and female, or they can shift between the genders.

The term "gender fluidity" describes how a person's gender identity, expression, or presentation can change over time or in different settings. This can happen to non-binary people. The variety of gender experiences is celebrated and gender norms are questioned by this fluidity.

Genderqueer and Gender Nonconforming: Some non-binary people reject gender norms and expectations from society by identifying as genderqueer or gender nonconforming when describing their gender identity.

Pronouns and identification: To express their gender identification and refute binary presumptions about gender, non-binary people can use a range of pronouns, such as they/them/theirs, xe/xem/xyrs, ze/hir/hirs, or other gender-neutral pronouns.

3. Issues and Validations: - Discrimination and Stigma: People who identify as transgender or non-binary frequently experience prejudice, societal hurdles, and discrimination because of their gender identification. This may have an effect on social acceptance, job, housing, healthcare access, mental health, and overall well-being.

The promotion of understanding, acceptance, and rights for transgender and non-binary people depends on increased visibility, representation, awareness, education, and advocacy initiatives. Gender diversity is affirmed through encouraging communities, inclusive legislation, and positive media representations.

The identities and experiences of transgender and non-binary people must be validated. This can be done in large part by affirming gender identity, providing allyship, friendly surroundings, healthcare that is gender affirming, and inclusive language and behaviors.

The Fourth Aspect of Intersectionality and Diversity: - Intersectional Identities: The experiences of transgender and non-binary people intersect with several dimensions of identity, such as race, ethnicity, culture, socioeconomic status, disability, sexual orientation, education, and more. Understanding the varied perspectives and needs of persons requires an awareness of intersectionality and its resolution.

Diverse Paths toward Self-Discovery, Affirmation, and Authenticity: Transgender and non-binary people have a variety of identities, experiences, and manifestations. Within communities and society, accepting this variety promotes empathy, inclusion, and respect.

To summarize, the experiences of those who identify as transgender or non-binary involve a wide range of identities, expressions, struggles, and affirmations across the gender variety continuum. Acknowledging and honoring people's gender identities, experiences, and rights is essential to establishing environments that are welcoming, affirming, and helpful to everyone, regardless of personal gender expression.

The intersections of mental health, sexuality, and gender:

Gender, sexuality, and mental health are interrelated and have complicated effects on each other's lives, experiences, and ability to access resources and support. This is known as the intersectionality of these issues. Addressing the various needs, difficulties, and capabilities of people in a variety of contexts and groups requires an understanding of intersectionality. Let's take a closer look at how gender, sexuality, and mental health intersect:

Gender identity and mental health: - Gender dysphoria: People who identify as transgender may suffer from this condition, which can lead to psychological issues, anxiety, depression, and other forms of suffering because of the mismatch between their assigned sex and gender identity.
- Social Stigma and Discrimination: Transgender and gender non-conforming people's mental health, self-esteem, identity development, and emotional well-being can all be adversely affected by stigma, discrimination, prejudice, and social exclusion based on gender identity.
- Affirmation and Support: Transgender people's mental health, resilience, and self-acceptance are greatly enhanced by gender-affirming activities including social transition, access to gender-affirming healthcare, supportive environments, and gender identity affirmation.

2. Sexual Orientation and Mental Health: - Minority Stress: People who identify as lesbian, gay, bisexual, and queer (LGBTQ+) may be stigmatized by society, face discrimination, rejection, become invisible, and internalize homophobia or biphobia. Anxiety, sadness, substance abuse, and suicidality are a few mental health issues that this stress may exacerbate.
- Coming Out Process: For LGBTQ+ people, coming out (i.e., declaring one's sexual orientation) can be a life-changing experience that affects their relationships, identity development, and social support systems.

- Supportive Environments: Having access to affirming healthcare, connecting with other LGBTQ+ people in the community, and receiving acceptance from friends, family, and society all help LGBTQ+ people achieve good mental health outcomes.

3. Intersectionality and Diversity: - Multiple Identities: People can identify as belonging to more than one identity depending on their age, gender, sexual orientation, race, ethnicity, culture, religion, socioeconomic level, handicap, and other characteristics. The experiences of discrimination, privilege, resiliency, and resource access are impacted by these overlapping identities.
- Marginalization and Resilience: People with intersectional identities may encounter social exclusion, marginalization, and differences in the consequences of their mental health. But people whose identities overlap also show strength, resilience, and cultural resources that support wellbeing and coping.
The recognition and resolution of intersectionality necessitates cultural competency, sensitivity, and understanding among mental health practitioners, healthcare providers, educators, legislators, and community organizations in order to offer inclusive and affirming services.

The issue of access to mental health care and support for individuals with diverse gender and sexual identities can be impeded by various factors such as stigma, discrimination, lack of culturally competent care, financial barriers, legal obstacles, geographic limitations, and systemic inequalities.
Adopting trauma-informed, LGBTQ+-affirming, culturally sensitive, and intersectional methods to assessment, diagnosis, treatment, and support services are all components of inclusive mental health practices. Using inclusive language, honoring identities and pronouns, removing structural obstacles, and advancing equity and accessibility are a few examples of this.
- Community Resources: Advocacy groups, LGBTQ+ community centers, peer support networks, helplines, internet resources, and community centers are essential in helping different communities receive mental health services that are affirming, culturally appropriate, and easily available.

5. Empowerment and Advocacy: - Self-Advocacy: It is crucial to enable people to speak up for their own needs, rights, and mental health. Promoting self-care,

resilience-building techniques, assertiveness training, and seeking out competent and affirming healthcare are all part of this.

Community Advocacy: Individuals with diverse gender and sexual identities can find more inclusive, supportive, and equitable environments through collective advocacy efforts, policy changes, anti-discrimination laws, inclusive education, destigmatization campaigns, and cultural awareness initiatives.

To summarize, the interplay between gender, sexuality, and mental health underscores the interdependence of varied identities, encounters, and obstacles encountered by members of marginalized communities. An all-encompassing, inclusive, and culturally competent strategy that supports fairness, dignity, empowerment, and resilience for every person regardless of gender identity or sexual orientation is needed to recognize and address intersectionality.

Problems and Shame Experiencing LGBTQ+ People:

Owing to cultural standards, discrimination, and lack of acceptance based on their gender identity, sexual orientation, or both, LGBTQ+ people experience a variety of difficulties and stigma. Their mental health, relationships, work, education, access to healthcare, and general well-being are just a few of the areas of their lives that may be impacted by these obstacles. LGBTQ+ people encounter the following major obstacles and types of stigma:

1. Discrimination and Social Stigma: Due to their gender identity or sexual orientation, LGBTQ+ people frequently experience discrimination, prejudice, and social stigma.
There are many ways that stigma can appear, such as hate speech, rejection, exclusion, rejection through words, and bullying.
- Discrimination may take place in public areas, businesses, educational institutions, housing, healthcare facilities, and judicial systems. As a result, victims may feel alone, afraid, and marginalized.

2. Acceptance and Rejection from Family: - Coming out to family members can be difficult, and LGBTQ+ people may experience hostility, rejection, or a lack of acceptance from family members.
. Difficult family ties, emotional discomfort, loneliness, and isolation can all be attributed to family rejection.
. Fostering mental health, resilience, and overall well-being among LGBTQ+ individuals is greatly aided by supportive and welcoming families.

3. Mental Health and Well-Being: Individuals who identify as LGBTQ+ are more likely than the overall population to experience mental health problems such depression, anxiety, substance abuse, self-harm, and suicidality.

- Mental health problems can be exacerbated by minority stress, internalized homophobia or transphobia, trauma, discrimination, social isolation, and a lack of social support.

To enhance mental health and resilience, it is crucial to have access to culturally competent mental health treatment, affirming therapy, support groups, and community resources.

Healthcare disparities: People who identify as LGBTQ+ may encounter obstacles while attempting to obtain healthcare services that are inclusive, affirming, and culturally sensitive.

. Healthcare disparities may be caused by prejudice, a lack of LGBTQ+ health professional education, gatekeeping, privacy issues, and difficulties getting access to reproductive or gender-affirming healthcare.

Reducing healthcare disparities requires training healthcare professionals, advocating for LGBTQ+-inclusive healthcare policy, and providing access to affirming treatment.

5. Legal and Policy Difficulties: - People who identify as LGBTQ+ may have legal difficulties with regard to job discrimination, housing discrimination, adoption, parenting rights, civil rights, and hate crimes.

. Barriers to full inclusion and equality and systemic inequities are caused by discriminatory policies, anti-LGBTQ+ laws, inadequate legal safeguards, and the nonrecognition of gender identity and relationships.

. Equal rights, protections, and dignity under the law must be advanced via advocacy campaigns, legislative changes, anti-discrimination legislation, and LGBTQ+ rights initiatives.

6. Workplace and educational environments: - In educational institutions, such as colleges and universities, LGBTQ+ people may encounter prejudice, harassment, bullying, and a lack of inclusivity.

- LGBTQ+ people's job prospects, career advancement, and job happiness can be negatively impacted by workplace discrimination, bigotry, microaggressions, and a lack of employment rights.

In order to create safer, more equitable, and affirming workplaces, it is recommended to create LGBTQ+ inclusive school curricula, anti-bullying policies, diversity training, workplace diversity programs, and inclusive hiring practices.

The term "intersectionality" describes the overlapping and intertwined nature of various dimensions of identity, including gender identity and sexual orientation, as well as race, ethnicity, culture, religion, disability, socioeconomic background, and immigrant status. The stigma, discrimination, and structural obstacles that LGBTQ+ people with intersecting marginalized identities may experience can exacerbate their vulnerability and make it more difficult for them to get resources and help. To advance equity, inclusiveness, and social justice within LGBTQ+ communities and larger society, it is imperative to acknowledge and address intersectionality.

The way LGBTQ+ individuals are portrayed in the media can reinforce negative stereotypes, misunderstandings, and stigmatizing stories, which can affect the general public's views, acceptance, and attitudes.

- Diverse and positive depictions of LGBTQ+ identities, relationships, and experiences in storytelling, entertainment, and the media help dispel preconceptions, increase visibility, and develop empathy and understanding.

It takes a team effort from society, institutions, the community, and each individual to address the issues and stigma LGBTQ+ people experience. The first stages in establishing safer, more just, and affirming environments for LGBTQ+ people to flourish and live authentically are promoting acceptance, inclusion, education, activism, legal protections, affirming healthcare, mental health assistance, and cultural transformation.

CHAPTER EIGHT:

Sexuality and Mental Health:

The two facets of human well-being—sexuality and mental health—are intertwined and have different effects on one another. Recognizing the intricacies, difficulties, and positive facets of sexual expression, identity, experiences, and attitudes is essential to understanding the connection between sexuality and mental health. The following are some important things to think about in relation to mental health and sexuality:

1. Sexuality as a Basic Aspect of Identity: - Sexuality is a multifaceted concept that includes sexual orientation, as well as desires, attractions, fantasies, behaviors, relationships, and values.
A person's sexual identity is an essential component of their total identity, supporting their sense of self, their level of self-worth, and their general well-being.

2. The Impact of Shame and Stigma: - Internalized negative ideas about one's sexual identity or experiences, shame, guilt, and secrecy can all be caused by stigma, discrimination, and cultural attitudes toward sexuality. Mental health, self-esteem, body image, and sexual satisfaction can all suffer from internalized shame and stigma around sexuality.

3. pleasant Aspects of Sexuality: Emotional closeness, pleasure, contentment, and general well-being can all be enhanced by healthy sexual expression, intimacy, and pleasant sexual encounters.
Positive sexual experiences and mental health advantages are enhanced by open communication, mutual consent, respect, trust, and intimacy in romantic partnerships.

Relationship dynamics and sexuality: - Intimate relationships, bonding, communication, trust, and emotional connection between partners are all greatly influenced by sexuality.

Stress, relationship unhappiness, and mental health problems can be exacerbated by difficulties in sexual interactions, sexual dysfunction, disagreements, or a lack of closeness.

5. Sexuality and Mental Health Challenges: - Abuse, coercion, or sexual trauma can have a significant negative impact on mental health, increasing the risk of depression, anxiety, and post-traumatic stress disorder (PTSD).

- Sexual dysfunctions can affect one's quality of life, relationships, mental health, and self-esteem. Examples of these include erectile dysfunction, low libido, early ejaculation, and sexual pain disorders.

Anxiety, depression, and other mental health illnesses can be exacerbated by poor body image, irrational expectations, performance anxiety, and sexuality-related social pressures.

6. LGBTQ+ Identities and Mental Health: - Due to stigma, discrimination, minority stress, coming out processes, familial rejection, and a lack of social support, LGBTQ+ people may experience particular mental health issues.

- Promoting mental health and well-being among LGBTQ+ people requires access to LGBTQ+-affirming mental health care, community support, advocacy initiatives, and inclusive settings.

Trauma and Healing: Recovering from prior sexual trauma, abuse, or traumatic events requires addressing them through trauma-informed therapy, support networks, and healing modalities.

- Trauma-informed care acknowledges the influence of trauma on mental health and places a strong emphasis on therapy partnerships that are safe, empowering, trustworthy, and collaborative.

Sexuality education and awareness: - A thorough education about sexuality contributes to positive sexual attitudes and behaviors by fostering understanding, consent, boundaries, healthy relationships, and informed decision-making.

Sex-positive, welcoming, and supporting settings can be established by raising awareness, lowering stigma, and encouraging candid discussions about sexuality and mental health.

Seeking Professional Assistance, Therapy, Counseling, or Support Groups Specialized in Sexual Health and Mental Well-Being are beneficial options for those facing difficulties connected to their sexuality and mental health.
 In order to treat sexual health issues and advance holistic well-being, it is imperative that people have access to affirming, nonjudgmental, and culturally competent mental health care.

In conclusion, mental health and sexuality are entwined facets of the human experience that need assistance, empathy, and knowledge. In order to support general well-being and sexual health for people as well as communities, it is important to promote good sexual attitudes, eliminate stigma and shame, cultivate healthy relationships, address trauma, and offer comprehensive mental health care.

Psychological Disorders Affecting Sexual Functioning:

The interdependent domains of sexuality and mental health have a variety of effects on one another. It's important to acknowledge the complexity, difficulties, and good aspects of sexual expression, identity, experiences, and attitudes in order to comprehend the relationship between sexuality and mental health. When it comes to sexuality and mental health, keep the following in mind:

1. Sexual orientation, wants, attractions, fantasies, behaviors, relationships, and values are all components of sexuality, which is a fundamental aspect of identity.
   . An individual's sexual identity is an essential component of their total identity, making a positive impact on their self-worth, wellbeing, and self-concept.

The effects of shame and stigma include: - Internalized negative views about one's sexual identity or experiences; - Shame, guilt, and secrecy; - Discrimination; and - Shame. Mental well-being, self-worth, body image, and sexual satisfaction can all suffer from internalized shame and stigma around sexuality.

3. Positive Aspects of Sexuality: - Emotional fulfillment, pleasure, and general well-being can be derived from healthy sexual expression, intimacy, and positive sexual encounters.
   Good sexual experiences and mental health advantages are enhanced by open communication, shared consent, respect, trust, and intimacy in romantic partnerships.

4. Sexuality and Relationship Dynamics: - There is a strong correlation between sexuality and bonding, communication, trust, and emotional attachment in close relationships.

. Relationship problems, stress, and mental health problems can be exacerbated by difficulties in the bedroom, sexual dysfunction, disagreements, or a lack of closeness.

5. Issues with Sexuality and Mental Health: - Neglect, abuse, coercion, or sexual trauma can have a significant negative impact on mental health, increasing the risk of anxiety, sadness, and post-traumatic stress disorder (PTSD).

A person's mental health, self-esteem, relationships, and quality of life can all be negatively impacted by sexual dysfunctions (such as erectile dysfunction, early ejaculation, low libido, and sexual pain disorders).

. Anxiety disorders, mood disorders, and other mental health problems can be exacerbated by poor body image, irrational expectations, performance anxiety, and social pressures associated with sexuality.

6. LGBTQ+ Identities and Mental Health: - As a result of stigma, discrimination, minority stress, coming out processes, family rejection, and a lack of social support, LGBTQ+ people may experience particular mental health issues.

To promote LGBTQ+ people's mental health and well-being, it is essential that they have access to LGBTQ+-affirming mental health services, as well as inclusive environments, community support, and advocacy efforts.

Trauma and Healing: - In order to promote resilience and mental health recovery, it is imperative to address prior sexual trauma, abuse, or traumatic experiences through trauma-informed treatment, support groups, and healing practices.

Understanding the effects of trauma on mental health, trauma-informed care places a strong emphasis on patient safety, self-determination, collaboration, and trust.

8. Sexuality Education and Awareness: - Good sexual attitudes and behaviors are influenced by comprehensive sexuality education, which raises awareness of sexuality and encourages knowledge, consent, boundaries, healthy relationships, and sexual health.

. Friendly, welcoming, and sex-positive workplaces can be established by raising awareness, lowering stigma, and encouraging candid discussions about sexuality and mental health.

Getting Help and Resources: - People who are having problems with their sexuality or mental health may find it helpful to get help from a professional, attend therapy or counseling sessions, or join support groups that focus on these topics.
. Handling sexual health issues and advancing overall well-being need having access to affirming, nonjudgmental, and culturally competent mental health care.

Conclusively, mental health and sexuality are interwoven facets of the human condition that necessitate comprehension, empathy, and assistance. In order to support general well-being and sexual health for people as well as communities, it is important to promote good sexual attitudes, eliminate stigma and shame, cultivate healthy relationships, address trauma, and provide comprehensive mental health care.

Trauma and Sexual Wellness:

Intimacy, relationships, sexual functioning, and general well-being are all impacted by trauma, which can have a significant impact on sexual health. Acknowledging the intricacies, consequences, obstacles, and therapeutic approaches in the framework of trauma-informed treatment is essential to comprehending the relationship between trauma and sexual health. Taking into account trauma and sexual health, remember the following important points:

1. Types of Trauma: - Experiences ranging from childhood maltreatment and neglect to sexual abuse, assault, harassment, and violence, accidents, natural catastrophes, exposure to combat, medical trauma, and other upsetting incidents can all lead to trauma.
. Experiences of coercion, harassment, exploitation, or other forms of sexual abuse that result in psychological, emotional, or physical distress are explicitly referred to as sexual trauma.

The effects of trauma on sexual health are multifaceted and can affect relationships, body image, arousal, enjoyment, satisfaction, intimacy, desire, and sexual functioning.
. When it comes to sexual health, common repercussions of trauma could be:
Erectile dysfunction, premature ejaculation, anorgasmia, low libido, vaginismus, dyspareunia, or sexual aversion are examples of sexual dysfunctions that trauma survivors may encounter.
- poor Body Image: Stress can lead to erroneous perceptions of one's body, humiliation, self-blame, self-criticism, and a poor body image, all of which can cause problems with sexual expression and confidence.
Issues with Intimacy: Individuals who have experienced trauma may encounter difficulties in forming healthy boundaries in relationships, communicating, trust, and emotional intimacy.
- Anxiety and PTSD: Anxiety disorders, panic attacks, flashbacks, intrusive memories linked to trauma, and post-traumatic stress disorder (PTSD) can alter sexual experiences and negatively affect one's sexual well-being.

3. Sexual Health Through Trauma-Informed Lenses:

In order to provide sensitive, sympathetic, and supportive care, it is necessary to acknowledge the effects of trauma on people's life, behaviors, beliefs, and relationships.

Safety, reliability, autonomy, choice, teamwork, empowerment, and cultural humility are important tenets of trauma-informed treatment while handling trauma-related issues.

Creating secure, accepting, and affirming spaces for trauma survivors to examine and deal with sexual issues, boundaries, triggers, and healing procedures is the main goal of trauma-informed approaches to sexual health.

4. Recovery and Healing: - The physical, emotional, psychological, and relational facets of well-being must all be addressed in a holistic, multifaceted approach to healing from sexual trauma.

- Trauma survivors can process trauma memories, lessen distressing symptoms, and enhance coping mechanisms with the aid of trauma-focused therapy, such as dialectical behavior therapy (DBT), eye movement desensitization and reprocessing (EMDR), cognitive-behavioral therapy (CBT), and trauma-focused cognitive processing therapy (TF-CBT).

. In addition to standard therapy, integrative approaches to healing can encourage comprehensive recovery. These techniques include mindfulness exercises, expressive arts therapies, body-centered treatments (including somatic experience), trauma-sensitive yoga, and peer support groups.

5. Communication and agreement: - Safe, consensual, and enjoyable sexual interactions are mostly dependent on open communication, mutual agreement, respect for limits, and explicit communication regarding sexual preferences, desires, worries, and triggers.

. With an emphasis on comfort, safety, and empowerment, trauma survivors may benefit from learning assertiveness techniques, self-advocacy tactics, and good communication patterns in sexual interactions.

6. Assistance and Materials: - Individuals who have experienced trauma can gain advantages from having access to peer support groups, crisis hotlines, sexual health clinics, trauma-informed mental health providers, and specialized support programs.
. Fostering environments that are supportive, inclusive, and powerful for trauma survivors requires educating healthcare professionals, educators, caregivers, and communities on trauma-informed care, trauma sensitivity, and sexual health advocacy.

In summary, sexual functioning, intimacy, relationships, and emotional experiences are all impacted by trauma, which has a major negative influence on sexual health and wellbeing. Safe, trustworthy, empowering, and healing are the main tenets of trauma-informed approaches to sexual health, which help trauma survivors heal and have healthy relationships. Improved sexual health outcomes and general well-being can be achieved by trauma survivors by making use of supporting services, trauma-informed care, and holistic healing techniques.

Resilience Techniques for Sexual and Mental Health Issues:

Managing issues related to one's sexual and mental health requires a comprehensive strategy that takes into account one's physical, emotional, psychological, and interpersonal well-being. Creating a coping strategy that is specific to each person's requirements, preferences, abilities, and resources is crucial. The following are some coping mechanisms for handling problems related to mental and sexual health:

To obtain professional assistance, speak with counselors, therapists, mental health specialists, or sex therapists who specialize in treating issues related to mental and sexual health.
- Attend counseling sessions, either one-on-one or in groups, with a focus on relationship problems, mindfulness, trauma recovery, sexual health, or stress management.

2. Awareness and Education: - Become knowledgeable about topics such as consent, boundaries, good relationships, mental and sexual health, trauma, communication techniques, and coping mechanisms.
"- If you want to learn more about sexual and mental health, take advantage of workshops, webinars, or educational programs.

3. Exercise and Take Care of Yourself: Make self-care activities that support your physical, emotional, and mental health a priority. These include mindfulness exercises, physical activity, enough sleep, a good diet, and relaxation methods.
- Take part in enjoyable, stress-relieving, and fulfilling activities; they could include reading, writing, taking nature walks, creative expression, hobbies, or quality time with loved ones.

Techniques for Mindfulness and Relaxation: To alleviate stress and encourage relaxation, try mindfulness meditation, progressive muscle relaxation, yoga, guided imagery, or deep breathing exercises.
To improve awareness of feelings, ideas, emotions, and triggers associated with issues with one's sexual and mental health, practice mindfulness.

5. Cognitive-Behavioral Strategies: Apply cognitive-behavioral methods to confront pessimistic ideas, convictions, and self-criticism concerning mental and sexual health problems.
- Learn coping mechanisms for handling upsetting feelings, adjusting to triggers, addressing problems, being assertive, and establishing reasonable objectives.

6. Healthy Coping Mechanisms: - Recognize and swap out unhealthy coping methods that undermine resilience and well-being, such as substance abuse, avoidance, and self-harm.
- Avoid harmful behaviors by participating in activities that support emotional regulation, self-expression, self-care, and self-compassion.

7. Develop Supportive Relationships: - Develop relationships of trust with dependable family members, friends, partners, or support groups that offer compassion, validation, understanding, and motivation.
Establish open and honest communication in relationships to promote closeness, trust, and a sense of connection regarding your needs, wants, and preferences.

8. Set Boundaries and Engage in Self-Advocacy: - To safeguard your mental, physical, and sexual health, set clear boundaries in social situations, professional settings, and romantic relationships.
- Work on your self-advocacy, self-assertion, and assertiveness skills when it comes to expressing your needs, preferences, and boundaries in different situations.

9. Take Part in Meaningful Activities: - Take part in endeavors that foster a feeling of accomplishment, significance, and community. Examples of these include community service, advocacy work, artistic endeavors, and volunteering.
- To improve overall life happiness and resilience, concentrate on activities that are in line with your values, interests, strengths, and aspirations.

10. Make Use of Supportive Resources: - Make use of resources like self-help books, mental health apps, crisis hotlines, online support groups, and neighborhood organizations that promote sexual health, trauma recovery, mental health, and general well-being.
Seek expert advice and recommendations for programs or services that effectively address particular sexual or mental health issues.

It's critical to keep in mind that coping mechanisms might differ from person to person, and it's acceptable to experiment with several techniques until you find the one that suits you the best. Effectively managing sexual and mental health difficulties and increasing overall well-being involves establishing healthy coping skills, obtaining professional help, prioritizing self-care, and building a strong support network.

The Value of Counseling and Therapy for Handling Sexual Issues:

By offering a secure, private, and encouraging setting for people to explore, comprehend, and resolve their worries, therapy and counseling are essential in resolving sexual disorders. Therapy provides a number of advantages that enhance sexual health and well-being, regardless of the issues it addresses, including sexual dysfunction, trauma, relationship difficulties, identity discovery, and other sexuality-related concerns. The following are some major arguments in favor of treatment and counseling for dealing with sexual issues:

1. Safe and Confidential Space: Individuals seeking therapy can speak candidly about delicate and private sexual issues without worrying about being judged, stigmatized, or having their privacy invaded.
- In a therapy atmosphere, clients can feel safe sharing their experiences, ideas, feelings, and difficulties surrounding their sexuality since it fosters trust, empathy, and nonjudgmental support.

2. investigation and Understanding: - Self-reflection, understanding, and investigation of one's sexuality, desires, values, beliefs, and experiences are all encouraged in therapy.
- Therapists work with clients to investigate the underlying causes of sexual problems, including traumas, relationship dynamics, self-concept, past experiences, and cultural influences.

3. Identifying and Addressing Concerns: - Therapists assist clients in recognizing and elucidating particular sexual concerns, such as sexual dysfunction (such as low libido, early ejaculation, or erectile dysfunction), sexual trauma, intimacy problems, body image problems, sexual orientation exploration, gender identity issues, or relationship conflicts.

- Therapists collaborate with their clients to create individualized therapy plans and tactics that effectively address their specific sexual disorders through assessment, psychoeducation, and collaborative goal-setting.

4. Trauma Recovery and Healing: - Therapy is crucial for people who have gone through sexual trauma, abuse, assault, or harassment because it offers a secure environment for processing, healing, and recovery from trauma.
- Trauma survivors can better manage painful symptoms, process trauma memories, and develop coping mechanisms with the support of trauma-informed therapy modalities such dialectical behavior therapy (DBT), eye movement desensitization and reprocessing (EMDR), cognitive-behavioral therapy (CBT), and somatic experience.

5. Improving Sexual Functioning: Using psychoeducation, behavior modification strategies, communication skills training, and cognitive restructuring, therapists assist clients in addressing sexual dysfunctions (such as erectile dysfunction, orgasm issues, pain disorders, and sexual aversion).
- Enhancing sexual satisfaction, intimacy, communication, and enjoyment is the goal of specialized treatment known as "sex therapy," which is beneficial for both individuals and couples. It focuses on sexual health and functioning.

6. Improving Relationships and Communication: - Counseling enhances assertiveness, conflict resolution techniques, and communication skills—all of which are essential for successfully negotiating sexual concerns, boundaries, consent, and relationship dynamics.
- Relationship counseling or couples therapy assists partners in resolving sexual issues, improving intimacy, reestablishing trust, and fortifying emotional bonds.

7. Encouraging Sexual Wellness and Health: - Psychoeducation on sexual wellness, safer sexual practices, contraception, STIs, consent, pleasure enhancement, and sexual self-care is given by therapists.
- Therapy encourages sexual empowerment, autonomy, and well-being by helping people to develop positive attitudes, beliefs, and actions linked to sexuality.

8. Fostering the Exploration of Sexual Orientation and Gender Identity: - Counseling provides a safe space for people to explore their gender identity, sexual orientation, or other elements of their sexuality.
- LGBTQ+-affirming therapists help people navigate identity acceptance, family relationships, community connections, coming out, and social acceptance by offering validation, support, resources, and direction.

9. Holistic Approach to Well-Being: - Counseling addresses the interdependence of the physical, emotional, psychological, social, and relational elements that affect sexual health and general wellness. This is known as a holistic approach to well-being.
- In order to promote overall sexual health and mental well-being, therapists work in tandem with their clients to incorporate coping mechanisms, self-care routines, stress management strategies, and healthy lifestyle adjustments.

10. Empowerment and Self-Discovery: - Counseling helps people achieve a positive sense of identity, agency, and confidence in managing their sexual lives. It also encourages empowerment, self-awareness, self-acceptance, and self-discovery.
- In order to overcome obstacles, make wise decisions, set boundaries, speak up for themselves, and create meaningful, gratifying relationships and sexual experiences, clients acquire the knowledge, skills, and resilience necessary to do these things.

In conclusion, therapy and counseling are vital tools for anyone looking for healing, direction, and support when dealing with sexual disorders. Therapy enhances sexual health, well-being, and general quality of life by fostering awareness, empowerment, resilience, and positive change through a collaborative and client-centered approach.

CHAPTER NINE

Sexuality, media, and technology:

Perceptions, attitudes, behaviors, and conversations around sexuality are greatly influenced by media and technology. How people connect, acquire information, express their sexuality, consume media content, and navigate sexual experiences has been impacted by the integration of media platforms, digital technologies, and internet sites. Key ideas illustrating how media, technology, and sexuality overlap are as follows:

1. Stereotypes in the Media: - The media, which includes books, music, movies, television shows, advertisements, and internet content, is a major influence in forming cultural norms, beauty standards, gender roles, and sexual expectations. Media portrayals of sexuality frequently reinforce objectification, sexualization, stereotypes, unrealistic standards, and limited depictions of the range of sexual identities, experiences, and orientations. In addition to dispelling myths, diversity, empathy, and more inclusive and affirming storylines surrounding sexuality, positive and inclusive media representation can also challenge stereotypes.

2. Sexual Education and Information Access: - Reproductive health services, consent education, sex education materials, and LGBTQ+ resources are all accessible through digital technologies and internet platforms.
. Anonymized, private, and inclusive learning possibilities for sexual health, relationships, pleasure, and consent are provided by online sex education programs, apps, websites, and virtual resources.

The way people communicate their sexuality, identities, relationships, and wants through images, videos, postings, and interactions is influenced by social media platforms.
. Diverse sexual communities can interact and become more empowered through social media's places for LGBTQ+ visibility, community development, advocacy, and support networks.

. Yet social media may also fuel peer pressure, cyberbullying, body image issues, sharing of sexual content, online abuse, and issues with digital permission as well as privacy hazards.

The rise of hookup culture and casual sexual encounters can be attributed to the way in which dating apps and internet platforms have revolutionized the way individuals interact, meet possible mates, and negotiate relationships.
. Virtual communication, sexting, online intimacy, and dating practices all have an impact on how people handle expectations, permission, boundaries, and sexual communication in online and offline relationships.

5. Pornography and Sexual Scripts: Young people in particular are affected by the widespread availability of online pornography, which has an effect on their sexual attitudes, thoughts, behaviors, and expectations.
. Consuming pornography can affect opinions about consent, body image standards, arousal patterns, sexual scripts, and attitudes about intimacy, sex, and relationships. Understanding how pornography affects sexual development, encouraging healthy sexuality, and dispelling myths or damaging ideas all depend on critical media literacy and thorough sex education.

Cyber-sex and Virtual Reality: - Through immersive experiences, interactive material, and virtual environments, digital technologies, virtual reality (VR), and augmented reality (AR) offer new pathways for exploring sexuality, intimacy, and sexual fantasies.
. Virtual communities, cybersex, online role-playing, and erotic content create concerns about consent, privacy, ethics, and boundaries that need for digital literacy and thoughtful thought.

Regarding permission, privacy, digital ethics, data security, and online safety in relation to sexual content, sexting, personal photos, and private messages, digital platforms and online interactions present significant issues.

. To encourage moral online behavior and avoid harm in online sexual contexts, education about digital consent, healthy boundaries, polite communication, online safety procedures, and legal rights is absolutely necessary.

The ability to critically analyze, dissect, and challenge media portrayals, messages, prejudices, biases, and influences pertaining to sexuality is crucial when it comes to media literacy and critical thinking.
- Developing media literacy skills enables people to make educated decisions about their sexual health, relationships, and media consumption as well as to interact critically with media content, question false narratives, and reject commercial pressures.

In conclusion, media and technology have a multifaceted impact on how people perceive and behave in connection to sexuality, influencing discussions about consent, identity, expression, and sexual health as well as relationships and conventions. Effectively negotiating the intersections of media, technology, and sexuality in a way that is morally sound, empowered, and informed requires fostering media literacy, digital ethics, inclusive representation, thorough sex education, and polite online interactions.

The impact of media on attitudes and behaviors related to sexuality:

Given that media platforms establish cultural norms, perceptions, ideas, values, and expectations connected to sexuality, media has a considerable impact on sexual attitudes and actions. People's perceptions, understandings, and expressions of their sexuality are greatly influenced by the media content they consume, which includes movies, TV series, advertisements, music, books, and social media. The media affects sexual attitudes and practices in the following major ways:

1. Sexual Norms and Values are Portrayed: Society's attitudes and actions about sexuality are shaped by the sexual norms, values, and expectations that the media frequently presents.
. Intimacy, sexual desire, gender roles, relationships, and beauty standards can all be influenced by the romanticized stories, idealized portrayals, and stereotypes found in media content.

2. Impact on Self-Esteem and Body Image: - People's judgments of their own bodies, their own worth, and their own idealized body types can all be influenced by media depictions, ads, and idealized body types, beauty standards, and sexual attractiveness.
Media representations of sexuality that are unrealistic in terms of appearance standards and sexual performance can lead to body dissatisfaction, peer pressure, and pressure to meet restricted beauty standards.

3. Normalization of Sexual acts and Attitudes: - By depicting particular sexual acts and attitudes as typical, desirable, acceptable, or expected, the media can mainstream them.

. Images in the media that depict casual sex, hookups, adultery, having numerous partners, and sexual experimentation may affect how people view and act in such ways.

The development of sexual scripts, or culturally taught patterns of sexual behaviors, roles, and expectations, is influenced by media narratives, storylines, and character portrayals.
Ideas about sexual scripts, role expectations, and relationship dynamics are shaped by media representations of romance, love, intimacy, consent, pleasure, and sexual communication.

5. Desensitization and Desensitization to Sexual Content: Excessive exposure to sexual content in the media, such as nude photos, sexualized ads, and sexually suggestive themes, can make people less sensitive to sexual stimuli and normalize the use of explicit content.
. How people view sexual desire, limits, consent, and the line separating imagination from reality in sexual relationships can all be impacted by desensitization.

6. Maintenance of Gender Stereotypes and Power Structures: - Stereotypes, disparities, and negative views toward gender and sexuality can be strengthened by media portrayals of gender roles, power structures, dominance, submission, and sex aggression.
Representations of sexual harassment, objectification, coercion, and gender-based violence in the media feed into harmful attitudes, beliefs, and actions around respect and consent in relationships.

The dissemination of safer sexual practices and knowledge on sexual health is facilitated by media outlets and public health initiatives. These efforts aim to raise awareness of HIV/AIDS, STI prevention, safer sexual practices, contraception, and consent.
. Adopting healthy sexual activities, seeking medical attention, and making educated decisions are all made possible by positive media messages, educational initiatives, and accurate sexual health information.

The impact of social media and online platforms on how people express, share, and consume sexual content, experiences, and narratives is a significant factor.
. Virtual communities, dating apps, sexting, and online interactions all influence how people negotiate sexuality in digital spaces by influencing digital sexual practices, communication patterns, and relationship dynamics.

The effects on adolescents and young adults are as follows: - Media exposure in these years can have a significant influence on sexual attitudes, beliefs, actions, and identity development. Encouraging young people to navigate media influences, question harmful ideas, and develop healthy sexual attitudes and practices requires critical thinking skills, comprehensive sex education, and media literacy instruction.

10. Cultural and Global Influence: - The media has a global impact on sexual attitudes and practices, influencing talks about sexuality in a variety of contexts and cultures as well as cultural changes and societal standards.
. On a worldwide scale, sexual views, values, and behaviors are influenced and negotiated through the use of digital media, global media platforms, and cross-cultural media exchanges.

In conclusion, impressions, expectations, ideals, and portrayals of sexuality are all shaped by the media, which has a considerable impact on sexual attitudes and actions. Healthy, knowledgeable, and respectful attitudes toward sexuality in society must be fostered by acknowledging the influence of media on sexual culture, developing media literacy, critical thinking, inclusive representation, and ethical media practices.

Online and Digital Trends in Sexuality:

Internet access, social media, digital technology, and online communities have all had an impact on a broad spectrum of developments, habits, and cultural shifts that are referred to as online and digital trends in sexuality. In the digital age, these tendencies have completely changed the way people explore, express, interact, and feel sexuality. These are a few significant digital and internet trends in sexuality:

1. The Culture of Online Hookup and Dating:

Social networking sites, dating apps, and online dating services have made it easier for those looking for romantic or sexual relationships to meet and communicate with one another.

- The emergence of casual sexual encounters, non-committal relationships, and hookup culture has been facilitated by digital dating platforms, which has affected people's understanding of intimacy, consent, and expectations in dating situations.

2. Digital Bonds and Digital Intimacy:

Digital communication technologies, video chats, and social media platforms have increased the prevalence of long-distance partnerships, virtual relationships, and online friendships.

- Practices related to online intimacy, like sexting, cybersex, virtual dates, and romantic encounters in virtual worlds, provide people who are geographically separated with alternate means of closeness and connection.

3. Expression of Sexuality on Social Media:

- Through images, videos, postings, stories, and interactions, social media platforms allow people to express their identities, relationships, sexuality, and wants.

Influencers on social media, bloggers, content producers, and celebrities all have an impact on sexual trends, beauty standards, and cultural norms through their online personas and content.

4. Education and Information on Sexual Health:

STI testing services, reproductive healthcare alternatives, materials for sex education, contraception, and information on sexual health are all accessible through websites, digital platforms, and online resources.

Initiatives for promoting safer sexual practices, consent education, and the de-stigmatization of sexual health issues are all facilitated by online sex education, including webinars, digital campaigns, and virtual seminars.

5. Augmented and virtual reality (VR/AR):

- Virtual reality porn, erotic content, interactive simulations, and digital intimacy encounters are just a few of the immersive sexuality-related experiences that VR and AR technology provide.

- Role-playing scenarios, virtual surroundings, and sexual exploration and pleasure are all made possible by VR platforms and applications.

6. Communities and Support Groups Online:

- People can share stories, ask for guidance, get support, and connect with others going through comparable issues linked to their sexual health or identity in online forums, support groups, and virtual communities.

LGBTQ+ online forums, communities, and social networking platforms help people with a range of sexual orientations and gender identities become more visible, advocate for themselves, and connect with others in similar situations.

7. Online Shopping and Products for Sexual Wellness:

Online shopping and discreet delivery are available for a variety of sexual wellness items, adult toys, lingerie, lubricants, contraception, and vitamins.

- A wide range of sexual tastes, kinks, fetishes, and interests are catered to by online markets and subscription services, which offer opportunities for self-care, experimentation, and sexual pleasure exploration.

8. Sexual Communication and Digital Consent:

Internet forums encourage conversations around digital consent, limits, proper sexting behavior, privacy settings, and courteous communication during virtual sex.

- Resources for managing moral, consensual, and courteous online sex encounters can be found in apps and applications that address consent management, tracking sexual wellness, intimacy coaching, and communication techniques.

9. Online Content Creation and Sex Work:

Through online sex employment and content development, people can profit from adult entertainment, webcam performances, OnlyFans subscriptions, and fan interactions through digital platforms.

- As the adult industry becomes more digitalized, questions concerning consent, safety, privacy, laws, and ethics are brought up.

10. Digital Awareness and Safer Internet Conduct:

- Resources, online safety policies, and education about digital literacy raise understanding of cybersecurity, privacy protection, identity and age verification, and online safety procedures in sexual contexts.

- The main goals of advocacy work are to stop harmful behaviors that affect people's wellbeing and online sexual encounters, such as cyberbullying, revenge porn, online harassment, and digital exploitation.

In conclusion, sexuality trends on the internet and in digital media are a reflection of changing patterns, attitudes, and societal changes brought about by digital platforms, online interactions, and digital technologies. In the digital age, these developments bring up issues of consent, privacy, safety, education, sexual expression, and ethics. They also present opportunities and problems. Achieving pleasant, consensual, and powerful sexual experiences and well-being through online and digital space navigation requires fostering digital literacy, responsible online conduct, inclusive representation, and informed decision-making.

Ethical Issues with How Sexuality Is Represented in the Media:

The promotion of responsible, courteous, and inclusive representations that respect human dignity, consent, privacy, diversity, and ethical norms depends heavily on ethical considerations in media portrayals of sexuality. The way society views, feels, believes, and behaves in relation to sexuality is greatly influenced by the media. Thus, ethical issues are crucial in guaranteeing that media representations represent a range of viewpoints, encourage informed consent, stay away from damaging stereotypes, and uphold the rights and autonomy of individuals. These are the main moral issues with how sexuality is portrayed in the media:

1. Informed Consent: - Media producers and creators should make it a top priority to get informed consent from anyone who is featured in sexual content, such as actors, models, and interview subjects or participants in documentaries. Transparent information regarding the content's intended use, any possible hazards, permissions, usage of photos or video, and the ability to revoke consent at any moment are all part of informed consent.

The media ought to make an effort to portray a range of sexual identities, orientations, gender expressions, body types, races, cultures, and abilities in order to prevent marginalization, exclusionary portrayals, or stereotypes.
"- In addition to being inclusive, genuine, and courteous, representation should also be free of damaging stereotypes, biases, and falsehoods that support stigmatization or discrimination.

3. Preventing Objectification and Exploitation: - Images of people that reduce them to objects of desire or that exploit or objectify people based on their sexual orientation or physical characteristics should not be used in media content.

- Objectification upholds negative beliefs, unfair power structures, and attitudes that are detrimental to human dignity, agency, and respect for people's rights and autonomy.

4. Consent in the Creation of Sexual Content: -Producers of adult entertainment and other sexual content should put an emphasis on moral production procedures, get performers' voluntary consent, make sure that they are fairly compensated, and respect their boundaries and general well-being. Emphasizing the value of ethical treatment and dignity in the creation of sexual material, consent should be continuous, explicit, freely provided, informed, enthusiastic, and reversible.

The delicate management of trauma and violence in the media requires careful attention to truth, sensitivity, and ethical considerations in order to prevent sensationalization, voyeuristic portrayals, or trauma being triggered by depictions of sexual trauma, violence, abuse, harassment, or exploitation.
Survivor-centered viewpoints, trauma-informed narrative, and responsible portrayals of delicate subjects connected to sexual abuse or violence have to be given top priority by content producers.

6. secrecy and Privacy: - When discussing personal experiences, tales, or information on sexuality, sexual health, or intimate relationships, media workers should respect people's right to secrecy, privacy, and consent. Maintaining moral standards in media representations requires staying away from sensationalism, invasive reporting, unapproved disclosures, and violations of private rights.

7. Preventing Harmful Stereotypes and Misinformation: - Content in the media should not reinforce negative preconceptions, myths, or false information regarding relationships, sexuality, gender roles, consent, sexuality, or sexual orientation.
- Accurate, inclusive depictions are promoted and harmful narratives are lessened through responsible reporting, fact-checking, diversity representation, and engaging with experts in sexual health and ethics.

8. Promoting critical thinking abilities, media literacy, and ethical education aids viewers in examining, challenging, and questioning media portrayals of sexuality, identifying prejudices, goals, and possible risks.
- People who are well-informed on consent, healthy relationships, sexual diversity, body positivity, and ethical media consumption are more equipped to resist harmful media practices and properly manage media influences.

9. Social Responsibility and Impact Awareness: - Media companies, platforms, and content producers have an obligation to weigh the possible effects of their work on the attitudes, actions, and sexual health of their target audiences.
- Media responsibility involves a number of crucial activities, including effect evaluations, communication with a variety of stakeholders, community consultation, and the promotion of constructive social change through moral storytelling and portrayal.

Media practitioners can maintain ethical standards, accountability, openness, and integrity in their work by adhering to ethical principles, industry standards, codes of conduct, and professional ethics frameworks.
- Engaging in cooperative efforts with ethics committees, professional associations, advocacy groups, and regulatory authorities fosters moral decision-making, discourse, and ongoing enhancement of media representations of sexuality.

In conclusion, ethical issues surrounding how sexuality is portrayed in the media highlight the significance of variety, accuracy, sensitivity, consent, respect, dignity, and social responsibility in developing media narratives, representations, and messages. Respecting morality creates inclusive media cultures, empowers viewers, and makes the conversation around sexuality in the media and society more fair, courteous, and knowledgeable.

Positive and Negative effects of Technology on Sexual Health:

The way individuals communicate, express themselves, obtain information, and manage many facets of life—including sexual health—has changed dramatically as a result of technology. Technology can have both positive and bad effects on people's sexual health, despite the fact that it affords a number of chances and benefits for boosting sexual health and well-being. The following are some advantages and disadvantages of technology for sexual health:

Benefits: 1. Information Accessibility
Good: Technology makes it simple to obtain current, reliable information about sexual health, including information on contraception, STI prevention, sexual anatomy, consent education, and reproductive health services.
Benefit: People can enhance their sexual health by being more knowledgeable, making wise decisions, and seeking out the right resources for healthcare.

2. Telemedicine and Online Consultations: - Positive: During the COVID-19 pandemic or in places with limited healthcare resources, telemedicine and online consultations enable people to obtain remote sexual health services, counseling, and advice.
Benefit: Improving accessibility and convenience encourages prompt interventions, screenings, care, and assistance for issues related to sexual health.

3. Kits for at-home STI testing:
- Positive: By providing people with discreet and easily accessible ways to buy HIV tests, STI testing kits, and at-home screening tools, online platforms enable people to monitor their sexual health in private.

Prompt treatment, early identification of STIs, and higher testing rates all contribute to STI prevention, lower transmission rates, and more public knowledge of sexual health issues.

4. Apps and Websites for Sexual Education:
Positive: Information about safe sex practices, consent, pleasure, reproductive health, and LGBTQ+ inclusivity may be found via interactive, interesting, and evidence-based sexual education apps, websites, and online resources.
Benefit: Having easy access to and thorough knowledge on sexuality fosters good attitudes regarding sexuality, healthy behaviors, and informed decision-making.

5. Networks of Digital Support:
- Proud: People can connect, exchange stories, look for guidance, and get peer support when it comes to difficulties with their sexual orientation, LGBTQ+ concerns, or relationship problems by using online support groups, forums, and communities.
Benefit: People are empowered, stigma is lessened, and mental health is promoted while managing sexual health difficulties when they have more social support, solidarity, validation, and advocacy.

Contraceptive apps and tools: - Positive: Menstrual cycle tracking, fertility monitoring, birth control reminders, and contraceptive tracking apps all assist people in taking charge of their reproductive health, effectively using contraception, and monitoring their fertility.
- Benefit: Better adherence to contraceptives, knowledgeable family planning choices, and individualized healthcare support the promotion of sexual health control, empowerment, and reproductive autonomy.

Drawbacks: 1. False information and inaccurate content
The internet and social media platforms have the potential to disseminate false information, myths, pseudoscience, and harmful attitudes regarding consent, STIs, sexual health, and reproductive rights.
- Risk: Improper information exposure can result in errors in perception, unsafe actions, inefficient procedures, and postponements in obtaining necessary medical care.

2. Sexual Harassment and Exploitation Online:
- Negative: The non-consensual sharing of private photos, grooming, cyberbullying, revenge porn, and sexual exploitation are all possible on online platforms.
- Risk: People's mental health, safety, and general well-being in online environments may be negatively impacted by injury, trauma, victimization, and privacy violations.

3. Digital Addiction and Distraction: - Bad: Overusing digital gadgets, social media, or online content can result in digital addiction, distraction, a decline in relationship intimacy, and a disregard for one's sexual health requirements.
- Risk: Stress, sleep disorders, communication problems, and a decrease in participation in activities that promote sexual health can all be attributed to unhealthy screen-time habits.

4. Privacy and Data Security Concerns: - Negative: Digital services, health apps, and online platforms may expose users to data breaches, personal sexual information exposure, and privacy issues such as unauthorized access to sensitive health information.
Risk: Information exploitation, privacy violations, data loss, and spying might damage confidence, discourage people from using online services for sexual health, or have unforeseen repercussions.

5. Digital Divide and Access restrictions: - Negative: A lack of digital literacy, restricted internet access, socioeconomic differences, or technological restrictions can all lead to unequal access to online resources, services, and information about sexual health.
- Risk: Accessing high-quality online sexual health assistance and interventions may be difficult for marginalized populations, such as low-income people, residents of rural areas, and underprivileged groups.

6. Safety Concerns and Dangers of Online Dating:
- Negative: Using hookup apps, online dating sites, and virtual interactions can put users at risk for harassment, unsafe encounters, sexual coercion, catfishing, and other crimes.
Danger: Insufficient authentication, inadequate safety measures, and anonymous communication can heighten susceptibility, undermine confidence, and result in unfavorable encounters during virtual sex or romantic relationships.

In summary, technology has a lot to give in terms of empowerment, sexual health, and information access, but it also has drawbacks and hazards that call for digital literacy, privacy protection, ethical thinking, and safe online behavior. Healthcare professionals, educators, legislators, digital platforms, and individuals must work together to address the detrimental effects of technology on sexual health and make sure that technology supports inclusive, equitable, and positive outcomes for everyone when it comes to sexual health.

CHAPTER TEN

Education and Advocacy on Sexuality:

Promoting informed choices, wholesome relationships, consent, sexual health, and overall well-being requires a strong emphasis on sexual education and advocacy. A wide range of projects, campaigns, programs, and activities are included in these efforts with the goal of promoting laws, rights, and resources that promote people's sexual health and rights and offering thorough, accurate, inclusive, and age-appropriate sexual education. Important facets of sexual activism and education are as follows:

Sexual Education:

1. All-inclusive Curriculum

- Create and implement thorough sexual education programs covering subjects like language skills, consent, healthy relationships, LGBTQ+ inclusivity, human anatomy, reproductive health, contraception, and STI prevention.

- To ensure relevance, engagement, and understanding, adapt instructional materials and methods to various age groups, cultural backgrounds, developmental stages, and learning preferences.

2. Information Drawn from Empirical Data:

- Give precise, factual, and scientifically supported information on topics such as safer sexual practices, contraception, gender identity, sexual orientation, consent, and enjoyment.

- Debunk falsehoods, raise awareness, and use education to dispel myths, misconceptions, stigma, and discrimination around sexuality, gender, and relationships.

3. Diversity and Inclusivity in Representation:

Make certain that all sexual education materials, tools, and conversations represent a range of identities, experiences, cultures, gender identities, sexual orientations, and relationships in order to foster inclusivity, respect, and understanding.

Adopt LGBTQ+ viewpoints, lingo, and experiences into sexual education programs to promote awareness, acceptance, and assistance for LGBTQ+ people.

4. Education of Consent:

- Stress the need of mutual agreement, enthusiastic consent, and the freedom to say no while teaching the principles of consent, boundaries, autonomy, respect, and communication in sexual encounters.

Training in assertive communication, active listening, identifying nonverbal clues, defining boundaries, and managing consent in many situations should be given.

5. Social Skills:

- Provide people the tools they need to create wholesome relationships, such as effective communication, empathy, trust, intimacy, self-awareness, and respect for others.

Discuss subjects including coercion, manipulation, emotional abuse, dating violence, and power dynamics in relationships while raising awareness and offering preventative and intervention techniques.

6. Services and Materials for Sexual Health:

- Inform people on how to get access to resources for counseling, HIV/AIDS prevention, STI testing, abortion services, sexual health services, and reproductive healthcare.

- Offer contact details for private counseling and resources available online, through hotlines, community organizations, healthcare providers, and sexual health clinics.

7. Cybersecurity and Digital Literacy:

Provide sexual education that includes digital literacy, privacy protection, online safety procedures, and critical media literacy to enable people to navigate digital environments, online relationships, and digital resources for sexual health in an ethical manner.

Handle hazards like sexting, digital consent, data privacy, cyberbullying, and online harassment as well as content exposure during online sexual encounters.

Advocacy:

1. Advocacy for policies:

- To guarantee that everyone has access to high-quality sexual education in contexts such as schools, communities, and healthcare facilities, national, state, and local advocates should push for comprehensive sexual education policies, curriculum standards, and guidelines.

Adopt laws that support gender equality, sexual health services, consent education, LGBTQ+ inclusivity, and rights-based approaches to sexuality education.

2. Educational Initiatives:

Advocate for sexual health, rights, consent, healthy relationships, stigma reduction, and the destigmatization of sexual diversity through public education campaigns, media outreach, and other means.

Leverage digital platforms, social media, narrative techniques, testimonies, films, infographics, and neighborhood gatherings to promote good attitudes regarding sexuality, dispel misconceptions, and engage a variety of audiences.

3. Participation in the Community:

Involve communities, parents, caregivers, educators, healthcare professionals, youth organizations, and advocacy groups in joint efforts to establish resources, enhance capacity, and promote sexual education.

Promote cooperation, communication, and partnerships to address cultural sensitivity, local needs, and obstacles to getting sexual health information and treatments.

4. Empowering Young People:

Youth-led advocacy, peer education initiatives, leadership training, and involvement in the formulation of health policies, sexual education curricula, and youth-friendly service offerings are all means by which to empower the youth.

Foster a more diverse, inclusive, and rights-based sexual education by elevating the voices, priorities, and experiences of young people.

5. Protections and Rights under Law:

- Promote legal rights, safeguards, and anti-discrimination legislation that protect people's liberties from exploitation, coercion, or violence; their right to privacy; their right to reproductive health; and their autonomous bodies.

- Encourage the repeal of laws that discriminate, advance gender equality, guarantee access to comprehensive sexual health care, and ensure that sexual education and advocacy adhere to human rights principles.

6. Approaches at the Intersection:

- Adopt intersectional approaches, which acknowledge how identities, vulnerabilities, and access to resources related to sexual health are shaped by a person's age, race, ethnicity, socioeconomic situation, disability, and immigrant status.

Advocacy initiatives that advance equity, social justice, and inclusion for underrepresented communities can help address disparities, institutional obstacles, and socioeconomic drivers of sexual health inequities.

In conclusion, supporting informed decision-making, empowerment, inclusivity, respect, and rights-based approaches to sexual health are all made possible by sexual education and advocacy. Sexual education and advocacy play a vital role in fostering healthier, more equitable, and respectful environments that enable everyone to thrive in their sexual health and well-being. They achieve this through promoting policies, educating the public, creating awareness, empowering individuals, and supporting communities.

Full Sexual Education's Significance:

To ensure that sexual rights are fulfilled, healthy relationships, informed decision-making, and sexual well-being are all supported, comprehensive sexual education is essential. A wide range of subjects pertaining to human sexuality, relationships, consent, diversity, gender identity, sexual orientation, pleasure, communication skills, and sexual health are covered, going beyond the most basic biological knowledge about reproduction. Key arguments supporting the significance of thorough sexual education are as follows:

1. Making Well-Informed Decisions: - Accurate, research-based information about STI prevention, sexual health, contraception, consent, pregnancy options, LGBTQ+ identities, and relationships is provided to people through comprehensive sexual education.

A person's ability to make decisions about relationships, healthcare services, contraception, and sexual activity is based on their values, preferences, and aspirations. This is known as informed decision-making.

2. Healthy Relationships: - Holistic sexual education teaches skills such as effective communication, empathy, mutual respect, setting boundaries, resolving conflicts, and comprehending consent that are necessary to create healthy relationships.

. Emotional well-being, less arguments, intimacy, and satisfying experiences in romantic and sexual relationships are all facilitated by an understanding of good relationship dynamics.

3. Consent and Boundaries: Comprehensive sexual education places a strong emphasis on the value of consent, boundaries, autonomy, and respect in all sexual encounters. It also stresses the need for open communication, mutual consent, and enthusiastic engagement.

. Conscientiousness education promotes favorable attitudes about polite, consensual sexual activity and aids in the prevention of sexual violence, harassment, and coercion from occurring.

The fourth area is sexual health and well-being. Comprehensive sexual education offers details on STI prevention, contraception options, frequent screenings, reproductive health care, and access to medical professionals.

. Improving overall sexual well-being, lowering STI rates, unintended pregnancies, and reproductive health disparities are all facilitated by promoting sexual health awareness, prevention techniques, and early intervention.

5. Inclusivity and Diversity: - A thorough sexual education program recognizes and celebrates a range of gender identities, expressions, sexual orientations, cultural origins, and relationship styles.

. Reduced stigma and discrimination are achieved through inclusive education, which supports visibility, acceptance, understanding, and respect for LGBTQ+ people, marginalized communities, and a range of sexual experiences.

6. Empowerment and Self-Esteem: All-inclusive sexual education helps people feel better about their bodies, their sexuality, and their self-worth. It also helps people become more self-aware and less ashamed of their sexual orientation and body image.

Giving people the tools they need to stand up for their rights, set limits, make educated decisions, and defend their sex rights promotes resilience, self-assurance, and empowerment when it comes to managing sexual experiences.

7. Reduction of Risks and Harms: - Comprehensive sexual education covers the risks of sexual engagement, including STIs, HIV/AIDS, unwanted pregnancy, sexual violence, coercion, exploitation, and internet hazards.

. Preventing harm, promoting safety, and defending people's sexual health and rights all depend on educating people about risk reduction techniques, safer sexual behaviors, healthy boundaries, and how to get support.

8. Social justice and equity: By addressing structural injustices, gender norms, power dynamics, discrimination, and obstacles to obtaining resources and services related to sexual health, comprehensive sexual education promotes social justice.

Encouraging equitable, rights-based sexual education helps advance reproductive justice, promote equity, combat stigma, and advance everyone's right to sexual freedom.

The promotion of open, honest, and developmentally appropriate communication about sexuality, relationships, consent, values, and personal beliefs between parents, caregivers, and children is a key component of comprehensive sexual education.

Fostering trust, understanding, advice, and supportive environments for discussing sexual health issues and working through obstacles together are all made possible by encouraging parent-child communication.

The implementation of comprehensive sexual education has been shown to yield favorable long-term health outcomes, such as decreased rates of unintended pregnancies, increased use of contraception, decreased rates of sexually transmitted infections, improved access to healthcare, and improved well-being over the course of an individual's lifetime.

Conclusively, thorough sexual education is essential for encouraging informed choices, wholesome partnerships, appreciation for diversity, self-determination, risk avoidance, and support of sexual injustice and rights. Comprehensive sexual education assists people in making informed decisions, managing sexual experiences responsibly, and reaching optimal sexual health and well-being by offering inclusive, accurate, age-appropriate, and rights-based information.

Advocacy for Sexual Health and Rights:

The promotion of laws, plans, and programs that protect people's rights to autonomy, sexual health, and reproductive health depends on advocacy for sexual health and rights. In order to effectively advocate for sexual health and rights, keep in mind these important tactics and focal points:

1. Advocating for policies that provide access to comprehensive sexual education in communities, healthcare facilities, and educational institutions is the first step.
Advocate for legislation that safeguards the right to an abortion, access to contraception, and healthcare for mothers.
- Encourage the implementation of laws that advance gender equality, LGBTQ+ rights, and nondiscrimination in public services, employment, and healthcare.

2. Educate and Raise Public Awareness : - Run public awareness campaigns on issues such as consent, sexual health, reproductive rights, positive relationships, and LGBTQ+ inclusivity.
. To break down stigma, dispel falsehoods, and encourage well-informed decision-making, provide factual information through workshops, seminars, and instructional materials.

3. Youth Empowerment: Through peer education programs, youth-led initiatives, and leadership development opportunities, young people are empowered to advocate for their sexual health and rights.
Support STI testing, confidential healthcare for teenagers and young adults, access to contraception, and youth-friendly services.

Involve communities, grassroots organizations, and civil society groups in order to address local needs related to sexual health, encourage communication, and motivate group action.

- Work together with religious leaders, community leaders, and cultural influencers to tackle harmful norms and behaviors while promoting acceptance and respecting diversity.

5. Healthcare Services and Accessibility: - Promote inclusive, affordable, and accessible sexual and reproductive health services, such as family planning, testing for sexually transmitted infections, HIV/AIDS prevention, STI treatment, and mental health assistance.
Providers should be trained in trauma-informed treatment, LGBTQ+ healthcare, cultural competence, and ethical standards around sexual health.

Sixth, Fighting Stigma and Discrimination: - Take up the fight against stigma, discrimination, and violence against marginalized groups, such as sex workers, LGBTQ+ persons, HIV/AIDS patients, and victims of sexual assault.
. To make healthcare settings safe and welcome for everyone, encourage inclusive language, protect privacy, and uphold confidentiality.

7. Lawful Advocacy: - Encourage legislative efforts to safeguard sexual autonomy, reproductive rights, and bodily integrity. This includes pushing for the decriminalization of adulterous consent, the abolition of coercive sterilization procedures, and other measures.
. Monitor and respond to abuses of sexual and reproductive rights, including forced marriage, child marriage, and gender-based violence, in collaboration with human rights organizations, advocacy groups, and legal professionals.

8. Media and Communication: - Advocate for policy reforms and societal norms that support sexual health and rights using media advocacy, social media campaigns, storytelling, and digital platforms. These strategies will help to increase awareness and elevate voices.
. Assist with the accurate, courteous, and inclusive coverage of sexual health topics and varied viewpoints by working with journalists, influencers, and media outlets.

The adoption of intersectional approaches is recommended to take into account the distinct needs and experiences of marginalized groups, such as individuals living in poverty, refugees, migrants, Indigenous communities, and persons with disabilities. Address structural barriers, socioeconomic determinants of health, and systematic injustices that affect people's access to sexual health resources, services, and rights.

10. International Advocacy and Partnerships: - Advocate for international agreements, conventions, and frameworks that safeguard gender equality, sexual autonomy, and reproductive rights as well as sexual health and rights as human rights.
Work together with global health initiatives, UN agencies, NGOs, and international organizations to fortify advocacy networks, exchange best practices, and push policy agendas that put sexual health and rights at the forefront of global concerns.

Advocacy groups can combat stigma and discrimination, promote the rights of all people to live healthy, meaningful lives, and create inclusive, rights-based approaches to sexual health by putting these advocacy strategies into practice and working with a variety of stakeholders.

Addressing Sexual Violence and Consent:

In order to protect people's safety, autonomy, and dignity during sexual encounters and relationships, it is imperative that sexual assault be addressed and consent is encouraged. In order to address sexual violence and encourage consent, the following are important tactics and approaches:

1. Education on Prevention:

1. Comprehensive Instruction on Sexuality:

- Put in place thorough sexual education programs that start at a young age and cover topics such as respectful behavior, healthy relationships, consent, and boundaries.

- Give age-appropriate instruction about the anatomy of the sex, reproductive health, contraception, STI prevention, and the value of consent and mutual respect in sexual relationships.

2. Consent Training and Workshops:

- To encourage awareness and application of affirmative consent, hold training sessions and workshops for students, youth organizations, parents, teachers, healthcare professionals, and community members.

Incorporate role-playing games, interactive exercises, and talks about negotiating limits, identifying indicators of consent, and accepting the autonomy and choices of others.

2. Encouraging Positive Consent:

1. Affirmative consent guidelines:

- Push for affirmative action rules that mandate clear, continuous, enthusiastic, voluntary consent in all sexual encounters in schools, colleges, companies, and community organizations.

To address cases of sexual misbehavior, harassment, or assault, promote the adoption of precise policies, codes of conduct, and reporting protocols.

2. Capabilities for Communication:

- Provide clear, courteous instruction on how to communicate desires, boundaries, and consent preferences in close relationships.

To guarantee mutual awareness and respect for one another's limits, place a strong emphasis on nonverbal indicators, active listening, empathy, and checking in with partners.

3. Sensitization and Protest:

1. Education and Awareness Programs:

To increase public awareness of sexual violence, consent culture, bystander intervention, and resources for survivors, start campaigns, social media campaigns, and neighborhood gatherings.

- Combat detrimental beliefs, myths, victim-blaming, and stereotypes that normalize coercive or non-consensual behavior and support the culture of rape.

2. Promoting Services and Policies:

- Push for laws that provide access to trauma-informed care, counseling services, legal assistance, and survivor-centered healthcare for victims of sexual assault.

Work together with advocacy groups, organizations, and legislators to enhance response procedures, boost financing for preventative initiatives, and reinforce offenders' accountability.

4. Assisting the Surviving:

1. Approaches that center on survivors:

- Support survivor-centered strategies that give survivors' independence, privacy, security, and welfare first priority during the reporting, disclosure, and decision-making phases.

Enable survivors to seek assistance, healing, and justice by providing them with confidential resources, crisis hotlines, support groups, and trauma-informed care.

2. Justice and Legal Assistance:

- Promote legislation changes that will give survivors' rights more protection in court, enhance the prosecution of sexual offenses, and increase access to justice.

Provide assistance to victims in resolving systemic obstacles to justice, navigating legal procedures, securing protective orders, and gaining access to victim compensation monies.

5. Social Media Involvement and Responsibility:

1. Civic Collaborations:

- Work together to develop coordinated responses to sexual violence that include accountability, support, and preventive strategies in partnership with local groups, healthcare providers, law enforcement, and leaders of the community.

- Use education, awareness, questioning damaging masculinity norms, and advocating for healthy masculinity to engage men and boys as allies in the fight against sexual assault.

2. Involvement of Bystanders:

- Train peers, community members, and bystanders on bystander intervention techniques so they can spot warning signals, step in safely, and assist those who may be sexually assaulted.

- Promote a culture of accountability, solidarity, and active bystandership in confronting and averting instances of sexual misconduct or coercion.

6. Persistent Advocacy and Policy Modification:

1. Reforming Policies:

The core causes of sexual violence, such as gender inequity, power disparities, cultural norms, and societal attitudes that support or tolerate sexual coercion, should be addressed by structural adjustments and policy reforms.

- Encourage campaigns that combat toxic masculinity, advance gender parity, confront the culture of rape, and cultivate contexts that value accountability, respect, and consent in all contexts.

2. Research and Data Collection:

- Assist in gathering information for evidence-based policies and interventions by sponsoring research projects, surveys, and data gathering activities on the prevalence of sexual violence, risk factors, experiences of survivors, and the efficacy of preventative measures.

Encourage the expansion of research on trauma recovery, consent education, sexual violence prevention, and best practices in survivor support services by advocating for funds, resources, and collaborations.

We can fight to create safer, more respectful workplaces that value consent, uphold the rights of survivors, and stop sexual violence in all its manifestations by putting these methods into practice and advocating for systemic, cultural, and policy changes.

Encouraging Healthy Practices in Sexuality:

Fostering healthy attitudes, behaviors, and relationships connected to sexuality, intimacy, and well-being requires promoting positive sexual health behaviors. The following are essential methods and techniques to encourage healthy sexual behavior:

1. Comprehensive Sexual Education: Establish comprehensive programs that educate people on sexual anatomy, reproductive health, contraception, STI prevention, consent, healthy relationships, and sexual pleasure in a way that is accurate, age-appropriate, and inclusive.
Incorporate conversations regarding sexual diversity, gender identity, sexual orientation, communication techniques, boundaries, and consent into sexual education programs offered to schools, universities, healthcare facilities, and community organizations.

2. Encourage Open Communication: - Promote honest, forthright, and nonjudgmental dialogue between partners, parents, caregivers, and medical professionals regarding sexual health, wants, boundaries, and expectations.
Encourage dialogue on topics such as pleasure, safer sexual practices, STI testing, contraception, consent, pregnancy planning, and relationship dynamics in order to build mutual respect, understanding, and trust.

3. Self-awareness and empowerment: - Provide people with the tools they need to make well-informed decisions about their sexual health and wellbeing in light of their needs, preferences, and beliefs.
Encourage people to embrace their bodies, communicate their desires, set limits, and stand up for themselves by promoting self-awareness, body positivity, self-esteem, and self-advocacy skills.

4. good Relationships: - Inform people about the qualities of a good relationship, such as equality, consent, dialogue, respect, empathy, and shared values.
- Offer training in dispute resolution, negotiation, active listening, and emotional intimacy to foster satisfying relationships and beneficial relationship dynamics.

5. Consent and Respect: - Encourage the development of a culture in which partners express explicit, voluntary, continuing, and enthusiastic consent before engaging in any sexual activity.
- Teach people how to read nonverbal clues, respect limits, and ask for verbal agreement when engaging in sexual activity to guarantee enjoyment and dignity for both parties.

6. Safer Sexual Practices: - Disseminate information and resources on safer sexual practices, such as consistent and appropriate condom use, STI testing, HPV and hepatitis vaccinations, and routine sexual health screenings.
- Promote conversations regarding techniques for reducing risk, condom negotiating tactics, dual protection techniques, and obtaining sexual health services for diagnosis, testing, and treatment.

7. Positive Body Image and Sexual Pleasure: - Dismantle stigma, shame, and unattainable beauty standards associated with bodies, sexuality, and sexual urges in order to promote positive body image, self-acceptance, and sexual self-esteem.
- Promote sexual gratification, sexual experience diversity, and exploration while stressing the value of intimacy, pleasure, and consent in sexual partnerships.

8. Diversity and Cultural competency: - Address a range of cultural views, values, customs, and beliefs about relationships and sexuality by including cultural sensitivity and competency into sexual health education and services.
- Acknowledge and honor a range of sexual orientations, gender identities, expressions, and interpersonal dynamics in order to promote LGBTQ+ communities and individuals with support and affirmation.

9. Affordable, nondiscriminatory, and easily available sexual health treatments that are inclusive of a range of identities and needs, culturally competent, and LGBTQ+ affirming should be promoted.
- Encourage programs that lower obstacles to sexual healthcare, such as prejudice, stigma, lack of knowledge, cost limitations, difficulty communicating in other languages, and restricted access in underprivileged areas.

10. Community Engagement and Support: - Involve communities, peer networks, support groups, and advocacy organizations in the dissemination of materials, the encouragement of healthy sexual activity, and the identification and meeting of local sexual health needs.
- Encourage collaborations with educators, legislators, healthcare professionals, and community leaders to lower stigma, improve access to resources and services for sexual health, and build supportive environments.

Through the promotion of positive sexual health behaviors through empowerment, inclusivity, education, and communication, we can help to foster a culture that values sexual well-being, enjoyment, consent, and respect for all people.

CHAPTER ELEVEN

Global and Cultural Views on Sexuality:

Diverse views, values, customs, behaviors, and attitudes toward relationships, gender roles, sexual expression, and sexual health are all part of the cultural and global perspectives on sexuality. These viewpoints fluctuate greatly among many communities, nations, and regions across the world and are influenced by cultural, historical, religious, social, and political influences. Here are some salient features of cultural and international views on sexuality:

First, Cultural Diversities

The range of cultural norms surrounding relationships and sexuality that exist throughout many nations and ethnic groups is referred to as cultural diversity.

Cultural variety affects how people feel about marriage, family structures, sexual norms, modesty, sexual education, sexual orientation, gender identity, and sexual activities.

2. Subjectivity to Culture:

Cultural relativism posits that cultural behaviors, values, and beliefs ought to be comprehended and assessed within their own cultural framework, as opposed to being measured against external benchmarks.

Regarding sexuality, morality, modesty, and sexual roles, cultural relativism recognizes that what is acceptable or forbidden in one culture may not be in another.

3. Influences of Religion:

- Cultural attitudes and conventions about gender roles, sexual ethics, marriage, contraception, abortion, sexuality, and family values are frequently shaped by religious beliefs and teachings.

There are differences in viewpoints toward sexuality, extramarital affairs, premarital sex, homosexuality, and reproductive rights across various religions, including Christianity, Islam, Judaism, Hinduism, Buddhism, and indigenous spiritual beliefs.

4. Expectations and Roles for Gender:

People's experiences with sexual health, relationships, and sexual expression are influenced by cultural norms and expectations surrounding gender roles, femininity, and sexual conduct.

- For men, women, and gender nonconforming people, traditional gender norms may limit their access to sexual education, healthcare, decision-making autonomy, reproductive choices, and sexual agency.

5. Community and Family Values:

- Cultural expectations surrounding sexual behavior, especially among young people, are shaped by family and community norms, which also influence views of sexuality, marriage, parenthood, virginity, premarital sex, and sexual modesty.

Individuals' autonomy, sexual expression, and access to sexual health information and services may be impacted by cultural beliefs pertaining to family honor, intergenerational relationships, arranged marriages, and parental control over sexuality.

6. Sexual Justice and Rights:

Global and cultural perspectives on sexual rights include freedom from violence, compulsion, and prejudice; sexual autonomy; physical integrity; consent; non-discrimination; reproductive rights; and gender equality.

- Promoting sexual rights as human rights, combating stigma, removing barriers based on culture, and fighting for inclusive laws, services, and safeguards for underprivileged groups of people are the main areas of focus for advocacy campaigns.

7. The Interaction of Globalization and Culture:

Diverse viewpoints on sexuality, gender identities, sexual behaviors, and relationships are shared across national boundaries and cultural boundaries as a result of globalization, migration, digital media, and cultural exchange.

How people and groups handle cultural variety, pluralism, and globalization's impact on sexual attitudes and practices is influenced by cultural hybridization, identity negotiation, and adaptability to shifting norms and values.

8. Sexual Practices and Health:

- Cultural customs, access to healthcare, education, and socioeconomic circumstances all influence cultural views and behaviors about sexual and reproductive health, contraception, STIs, HIV/AIDS prevention, family planning, birthing, and sexual healthcare. These variations are significant.

People's experiences, activities, and attitudes toward sexual health and well-being are influenced by cultural ideas on sexual pleasure, intimacy, sexual dysfunction, fertility, menstruation, menopause, and aging.

9. Difficulties and Disputations

Human rights, cultural relativism, sexual diversity, gender equity, LGBTQ+ rights, sex education, reproductive justice, and the prevention of sexual assault are some of the issues, debates, and conflicts that arise when considering sexuality from cultural and global perspectives.

- Through encouraging discussion, appreciating cultural subtleties, appreciating variety, opposing harmful practices, and arguing in favor of rights-based approaches to sexual health and rights, advocacy activities aim to negotiate these difficulties.

In conclusion, there are many different and intricate cultural and worldwide viewpoints on sexuality that are influenced by social, political, religious, and historical circumstances. Achieving human rights, dignity, and respect for everyone's sexuality requires an understanding of and respect for cultural diversity, the removal of barriers across cultural divides, the advancement of sexual rights, and the development of inclusive approaches to sexual health and well-being.

Sexual Norms and Practices Vary by Culture:

Different sexuality-related beliefs, values, attitudes, behaviors, and customs among countries, groups, and communities are referred to as cultural variances in sexual norms and practices. This rich tapestry of sexual diversity across the globe is woven by these variances, which are impacted by historical, religious, social, economic, and political influences. Cultural differences in sexual norms and practices can be seen in the following ways:

1. Attitudes Toward Virginity and Purity: - The cultural concepts of purity, honor, and family reputation can stigmatize or discourage premarital sex, especially for women. In many societies, virginity is highly esteemed. Some cultures might see premarital sex as a normal aspect of personal discovery and human development, while others might have more laxer views.

2. Values of Marriage and Families: - There are many different cultural conventions around marriage, monogamy, and family arrangements. Some cultures place a strong emphasis on planned weddings, large families, and gender roles that are customary.
. Diverse relationship models, such as same-sex unions, consensual non-monogamy, polyamory, and unconventional family structures, may be accepted in different cultures, in contrast.

3. Gender roles and sexual expression: - How people negotiate gender roles, sexual urges, and relationships is influenced by cultural expectations surrounding masculinity, femininity, and sexual expression.
. While some cultures support fluidity, gender diversity, and non-binary identities, others may have strict gender norms that regulate acceptable forms of sexual expression based on biological sex.

4. Sexual Education and Health Practices: Individuals' access to resources, knowledge, and healthcare is impacted by cultural attitudes and practices

surrounding sexual education, contraception, STI prevention, reproductive health, and sexual healthcare services.

. Open communication, access to resources, and discrepancies in sexual health outcomes can all be hampered by cultural taboos, shame, or false information regarding sexual health.

5. Sexual Taboos and Forbidden Practices: -There are cultural taboos surrounding specific sexual identities, behaviors, or practices that may be deemed improper, immoral, or unlawful according to cultural or religious beliefs.

. Taboos around homosexuality, body dysmorphic disorder (BDSM), sex work, masturbation, nudity, public gestures of affection, and non-heteronormative sexual identities and expressions are a few examples.

6. Sexual Rituals and customs: Reflecting cultural values, beliefs, and social conventions, many societies have rituals, ceremonies, or customs pertaining to sexuality, fertility, courting, marriage, and coming-of-age ceremonies. These activities could be genital mutilations, wedding traditions, menstrual taboos, fertility ceremonies, initiation rites, bridal virginity tests, or sexual acts associated with spiritual or religious beliefs.

7. Perceptions of Sexual enjoyment and Intimacy: - According to certain cultures, communication, emotional connection, and reciprocal enjoyment are important aspects of sexual interactions. These perceptions are influenced by cultural norms. Some cultures place more value on sexuality's spiritual, familial, or reproductive aspects and consider pleasure to be secondary or private.

8. Sexual Consent and Coercion: - Affirmative consent, mutual respect, and open communication are valued in certain cultures, while others place a higher emphasis on coercion, limits, and sexual consent.

. Cultural standards may tolerate or justify non-consensual relationship behaviors, marital rape, or coerced sexual behavior.

The ninth factor that shapes societal ideas about sexuality, marriage, procreation, contraception, abortion, LGBTQ+ identities, and sexual ethics is religion and spirituality.

. Sexual norms, behaviors, and moral standards are viewed differently by various religions, including Christianity, Islam, Judaism, Hinduism, Buddhism, and indigenous spiritual traditions.

10. Globalization and Cultural Exchange: These factors, together with migration, digital media, and globalization, push back against established cultural borders and promote cultural hybridization by spreading ideas, values, and conventions related to sexuality. Cultures can alter and engage in discussions and agreements about sexual diversity and rights when new sexual norms, practices, identities, and attitudes arise from cross-cultural interactions.

The promotion of human rights, dignity, and autonomy in sexual expression, relationships, and health is crucial, as is the recognition and appreciation of cultural differences in sexual norms and practices. In order to address disparities, challenge stigma, and promote healthy sexual experiences for people and communities worldwide, it is imperative that one understand cultural contexts, engage in culturally competent practices, and advocate for inclusive, rights-based sexual health and rights.

Global Difficulties Sexual Health:

Global sexual health difficulties include a variety of intricate problems that have an impact on people, groups, and cultures all across the world. Many variables, including cultural norms, socioeconomic gaps, gender inequality, access to healthcare, education, discrimination, stigma, and human rights violations, influence these difficulties. A multifaceted strategy including activism, education, healthcare services, regulatory reforms, and community involvement is needed to address these issues. These are a few of the major issues facing sexual health globally:

1. AIDS, HIV, and STI Epidemic:

- There is still much work to be done to combat the ongoing HIV/AIDS epidemic worldwide, especially in areas with high prevalence rates, restricted access to preventive measures like condoms and PrEP, and stigma associated with status.

Eliminating the stigma attached to HIV/AIDS is essential to lowering the number of new infections, enhancing health outcomes, and removing obstacles to HIV testing, treatment, care, and support services.

2. Health Disparities in Reproduction:

- Preventable maternal mortality, unwanted pregnancies, and unsafe abortions are caused in part by disparities in access to reproductive health services, such as family planning, contraception, maternal healthcare, and safe abortion services.

In order to improve mother and child health outcomes and reduce inequities, it is imperative to promote universal access to reproductive health services, comprehensive sexual education, and reproductive rights.

3. Violence Based on Gender:

- Gender-based violence, which affects people of all ages, genders, and backgrounds, is still a widespread global issue. It includes intimate relationship abuse, child marriage, female genital mutilation (FGM), sexual assault, and human trafficking.

In order to address gender-based violence and advance gender equality, it is imperative that preventive initiatives, survivor support programs, legislative safeguards, and community interventions be strengthened.

4. Rights to Procreation and Sexuality:

Maintaining an individual's autonomy, dignity, and capacity to make decisions about their bodies, sexual orientation, and reproductive choices depends on the sexual and reproductive rights being upheld as human rights.

Promoting comprehensive sexuality education, abortion rights, LGBTQ+ rights, access to contraception, and reproductive justice are essential for the advancement of sexual and reproductive health and rights worldwide.

5. Sexual Health in Youth:

Teenagers and young adults encounter particular difficulties with regard to sexual health, such as early pregnancy, STIs, lack of access to sexual education, peer pressure, and societal stigma.

To encourage good sexual health outcomes in young people, funding for youth-friendly sexual health services, peer education initiatives, thorough sexuality education, and mental health assistance is essential.

6. Concerning Sexual Health in Marginalized Groups:

- Access to sexual health services and information is frequently hampered for marginalized populations, such as sex workers, LGBTQ+ persons, people with disabilities, refugees, migrants, indigenous communities, and those experiencing humanitarian crises. These groups also frequently suffer prejudice and stigma.

Encouraging inclusivity, culturally sensitive healthcare, nondiscriminatory legislation, and community-led interventions is essential to meeting underrepresented communities' needs for sexual health and minimizing health disparities.

7. Issues with Technology and Digital Health:

Both opportunities and obstacles for sexual health are brought about by the digital environment, including the dissemination of harmful content, misinformation, online abuse, privacy issues, and access to telemedicine.

To leverage technology for positive results related to sexual health, it is imperative to promote responsible digital health behaviors, ethical technology usage in sexual health education and services, online safety measures, and digital literacy programs.

8. Increasing Risks to Sexual Health:

New infectious diseases, drug-resistant strains, the effects of climate change on reproductive health, dangers associated with cybersexual health, and antibiotic resistance in STIs are just a few examples of the emerging threats to sexual health that call for continued research, surveillance, and public health measures.

Healthcare professionals, researchers, legislators, and communities must work together to address new issues related to sexual health, respond to changing risks, and build readiness and resilience.

9. Global Pandemic Security and Health Security:

Global health crises can impair access to necessary services, disrupt healthcare systems, and worsen pre-existing sexual health issues. Examples of these crises include pandemics (like COVID-19), natural disasters, humanitarian crises, and armed wars.

Reducing the negative consequences of global health crises on sexual health requires bolstering health systems, guaranteeing the availability of sexual health services in an emergency, addressing socioeconomic repercussions, and advancing fairness in healthcare access.

10. Customs and Social Standards:

Deeply rooted taboos, cultural and societal standards, and beliefs about gender roles, virginity, consent, and sexual practices can have an impact on people's experiences, decisions, and access to treatments related to their sexual health.

- It is crucial to support rights-based approaches to sexual health education and services, courteous dialogue, cultural awareness, and community engagement while managing cultural challenges and advancing positive sexual health outcomes worldwide.

Conclusively, tackling worldwide issues related to sexual health necessitates an all-encompassing strategy that targets systemic injustices, advances human rights, gives individuals agency, involves communities, and cultivates cooperation between local, national, and global stakeholders. We may strive toward achieving equitable, inclusive, and rights-based sexual health outcomes for every person worldwide by giving evidence-based interventions first priority, advocating for policy reforms, investing in healthcare infrastructure, and providing comprehensive sexual health education.

Research on Sexuality Across Cultures:

Research on sexuality that crosses cultural boundaries examines and contrasts sexual norms, behaviors, attitudes, and beliefs between various nations, cultures, and geographical areas. This kind of study aids in the comprehension of the ways in which cultural contexts impact sexual practices, gender roles, sexual orientation, reproductive health, and sexual health outcomes, among other facets of sexuality. Important factors and methods in cross-cultural studies of sexuality are as follows:

1. Cultural Awareness and Deference:

- Cross-cultural studies on sexuality need researchers to approach the subject with cultural sensitivity, respect for differing viewpoints, and awareness of any prejudices or stereotypes.

The research's cultural relevance, validity, and ethical considerations can all be improved by working with local experts, community members, and cultural advisers.

2. Analysis of Comparisons:

In order to detect patterns, variandes, similarities, and differences in sexual attitudes, actions, and norms, cross-cultural researchers compare data and findings from various cultural contexts.

- Comprehensive insights on cross-cultural differences in sexuality can be obtained through the use of standardized measures, qualitative interviews, surveys, ethnographic methods, or mixed-methods approaches.

3. The Cultural Aspects of Sexuality:

- Scholars investigate the cultural factors—religious convictions, customs, social conventions, gender roles, familial values, media representations, and historical settings—that impact sexuality.

Researchers can better understand the intersections between culture and sexuality by identifying the cultural elements that influence sexual practices, identities, and health effects.

4. Sexual Attitudes and Customs:

- Studies examining similarities and variations between cultures with regard to sexual practices, behaviors, and customs include views toward premarital sex, the use of contraception, sexual education, the age of sexual initiation, and taboos.

Variations in sexual frequency, enjoyment, communication, and actions related to pursuing sexual health between cultures may also be the subject of research.

5. Gender Identity and Sexual Profession:

Researchers look at cultural expectations and conventions around gender roles, sexual orientation expression, and masculinity and femininity. They also look at attitudes toward same-sex couples, LGBTQ+ people, and non-binary identities.

Research may examine how LGBTQ+ people's experiences are impacted by social support networks, legal frameworks, discrimination, and cultural acceptability in various contexts.

6. Rights and Health in Reproduction:

Examining cultural views, behaviors, and laws pertaining to family planning, abortion, infertility, delivery, and reproductive rights is a key component of cross-cultural study on sexuality.

Interventions and policies aimed at improving sexual and reproductive health outcomes are informed by an understanding of the cultural impacts on reproductive decision-making, attitudes about reproductive technologies, access to services, and use of contraception.

7. Modernization and Globalization's Effects:

- New concepts, beliefs, media representations, and technological advancements brought about by modernity, migration, globalization, and cultural interchange have an impact on sexual norms, identities, and behaviors.

The effects of globalization on sexual attitudes, the sexualization of society, digital sexuality trends, cultural hybridization, and the ability to adjust to shifting sexual standards may all be studied in future research.

8. Interventions and Health Disparities:

Studies examining health disparities, inequality, and obstacles to resources, education, and services related to sexual health, particularly for marginalized communities, indigenous people, immigrants, refugees, and socioeconomically disadvantaged groups, are conducted across cultural boundaries.

- Determining best practices, culturally appropriate strategies, and successful interventions for promoting sexual health in a variety of cultural contexts aids in the reduction of inequities and enhancement of health outcomes.

9. Moral Points to Bear in Mind:

- To guarantee participant safety, privacy, and respect for cultural values, researchers doing cross-cultural study on sexuality must abide by ethical criteria, informed consent processes, confidentiality requirements, and cultural protocols.

Avoiding cultural appropriation, honoring indigenous knowledge, getting community agreement, and recognizing potential power imbalances in research partnerships are more ethical considerations.

10. Collaboration and Knowledge Exchange:

Researchers, practitioners, policymakers, community organizations, and cultural stakeholders can all benefit from information exchange, collaboration, and partnerships in cross-cultural study on sexuality.

Enhancing the effect and relevance of cross-cultural research outcomes involves sharing best practices, doing participatory research, incorporating community members in study design, and distributing findings in ways that are culturally appropriate.

Cross-cultural research on sexuality advances global efforts to promote sexual health, diversity, and rights for all people by taking a culturally sensitive, comparative approach and addressing ethical issues. It also adds to a deeper understanding of the influences of culture on sexuality, informs evidence-based interventions, and fosters cultural competence.

Techniques for Encouraging Sexual Health Equity:

Encouraging sexual health equity include tackling inequities, gaps, and injustices that impede people's access to resources, rights, and information on sexual health. A holistic strategy that tackles institutional obstacles, cultural variables, stigma, discrimination, and structural disparities as well as social determinants of health is necessary. To encourage parity in sexual health, consider the following tactics:

Adopt a paradigm for health equality that acknowledges the influence of social determinants of health (such as housing, employment, education, and sexual orientation) on sexual health outcomes, as well as race and ethnicity, gender identity, and sexual orientation.
. To achieve equity in sexual health, it is imperative to tackle the underlying social, economic, and environmental causes that give rise to health disparities.

2. Intersectional Approach: - Acknowledge how access to sexual health services, stigma, discrimination, and health outcomes are influenced by intersecting identities and experiences (such as race, ethnicity, gender, sexual orientation, disability, and immigrant status).
To achieve sexual health equality, adopt an intersectional perspective that takes into account experiences of marginalization and discrimination as well as many facets of identity.

In order to guarantee that sexual health treatments, information, and interventions are inclusive, courteous, and sensitive to cultural differences, it is important to foster cultural competency among healthcare professionals, educators, legislators, and community leaders.
Make sure that outreach, counseling, and education about sexual health include cultural sensitivity training, language access services, and culturally appropriate methods.

4. Comprehensive Sexual Education: - Promote inclusive, age-appropriate, evidence-based programs that address a range of sexual orientations, gender

identities, relationships, consent, pleasure, and reproductive health. We should also push for these programs.

Make sure that curricula on sexual education encourage respect for many identities and experiences, critical thinking, skill development, communication, and decision-making.

5. Access to Sexual Health Services: - Broaden the range of cheap, easily available, and inclusive sexual health services available, such as family planning, HIV/AIDS prevention, STI testing, contraception, mental health assistance, and LGBTQ+ affirming care.

- Take action against access obstacles include language hurdles, cultural stigma, lack of sexual health professional training, transportation inequalities, cost, insurance coverage, and geographic inequalities.

6. Community Empowerment and Community Engagement: - Involve communities, grassroots organizations, advocacy groups, and peer networks in the development, execution, and assessment of policies, programs, and interventions related to sexual health.

Provide communities and individuals with the tools they need to take up issues of stigma, discrimination, and injustice, access resources, and advocate for their rights related to sexual health.

Promote health literacy and empowerment by giving people of all ages, backgrounds, and abilities accurate, easily accessible, and culturally appropriate sexual health information, skills, and resources.

To reach marginalized people and encourage informed decision-making, employ a variety of communication channels, multimedia platforms, peer education, and community outreach techniques.

8. Reform and Advocacy for Policies: - Push for legislation that support sexual health equity, such as those that prohibit discrimination, safeguard reproductive rights, affirm LGBTQ+ rights, gender parity, and require universal access to comprehensive sexuality education.

. Work together with legislators, government agencies, civil society organizations, and politicians to distribute resources to underprivileged communities, overcome systemic impediments, and advance evidence-based initiatives.

9. Address discrimination and stigma around a variety of marginalized identities and experiences, such as sex work, HIV/AIDS, STIs, gender identity, sexual orientation, and reproductive choices.
To combat stereotypes, foster empathy, and establish welcoming environments that encourage sexual health equity, support anti-stigma campaigns, education programs, media literacy, and community discussions.

10. Data collection and monitoring: - Gather de-identified data on sexual health indicators (e.g., STI rates, use of contraceptives, reproductive outcomes) by demographic factors (e.g., age, race, ethnicity, sexual orientation, gender identity) in order to track advancements toward goals of sexual health equity and identify gaps.
Employ data-driven methods to guide choices about programs, policies, and resource distribution. This will help to meet individual needs and lessen inequalities in the outcomes of sexual health.

We may strive toward attaining sexual health equity for all people, regardless of their backgrounds, identities, or situations, by putting these methods into practice, working with stakeholders, lobbying for legislative reforms, and tackling the core causes of sexual health disparities.

CHAPTER TWELVE

Future Tendencies in Sexual Psychology:

In order to forecast future developments in sexual psychology, one must take into account new fields of study, developments in technology, alterations in culture and society, and changing views on human sexuality. The area of sexual psychology is anticipated to be shaped in the upcoming years by a number of significant trends and advancements, notwithstanding the inherent uncertainty of the future:

1. Technology and Virtual Closeness:

- The continued use of teledildonics, virtual reality (VR), augmented reality (AR), and online dating platforms in sexual encounters will impact people's perceptions of intimacy, sexual desire, and relationships.

The effects of digital intimacy on consent, privacy, cybersexuality, and sexual behavior may be the subject of research, as well as the creation of novel therapeutic therapies and instructional materials.

2. Well-being and Sexual Health:

- A growing focus on the importance of holistic sexual health, fulfilling sexual encounters, pleasure, and sexual well-being as constituents of general wellbeing and mental health.

Interventions, mindfulness exercises, sexual self-care techniques, and tailored ways to support resilience and sexual health throughout life may all be investigated in future research.

3. Varying Orientations and Sexual Identities:

Research on LGBTQ+ sexuality, non-binary experiences, asexuality, and gender-affirming treatment has expanded as a result of greater visibility, acceptance, and affirmation of varied sexual identities, orientations, and gender expressions.

Examination of the effects that legislative safeguards, cultural norms, societal attitudes, and healthcare access have on the relationships, mental health, and sexual pleasure of sexual minorities.

Intersectionality and Inclusivity in Practice:

- The recognition of the intricate interactions between many identities (such as race, ethnicity, gender, sexual orientation, disability, and socioeconomic status) and their impact on sexual experiences, identities, and resource accessibility is reflected in intersectional approaches in sexual psychology research.

- Fighting for equitable access to sexual health services by promoting inclusive practices, culturally sensitive care, and trauma-informed methods that address inequalities, prejudice, and obstacles.

5. Boundaries, Communication, and Consent:

Affirmative consent, sexual limits, effective communication, and positive relationship dynamics will all continue to be important topics in sexual psychology research, instruction, and clinical settings.

Examining digital technologies for consent, bystander intervention programs, consent education, and therapeutic approaches to sexual trauma, coercion, and power dynamics in partnerships.

6. Cultural Diversity and Global Views:

Enhancing global health programs, cross-cultural research partnerships, and culturally aware methods for comprehending sexual norms, behaviors, beliefs, and attitudes in many cultural situations.

Examining the ways in which migration, digital media, globalization, and cultural interchange affect sexual identities, values, and behaviors throughout the world.

7. Prevention and Education about Sexuality:

The development of comprehensive sexuality education, evidence-based programs for educating about sexuality, and preventative measures against STIs, HIV/AIDS, unwanted pregnancies, sexual violence, and disparities in sexual health.

- Using gamification, interactive platforms, digital tools, and peer education methods to improve sexual health literacy, skill development, and behavior modification across a range of demographics.

8. Sexual Joy and Longing:

- Studies on the relationship between psychological variables (such as fantasy, emotions, and cognition) and sexual experiences; they include pleasure, desire, arousal patterns, variability in sexual response, and individual differences in sexual preferences.

Investigating the lifetime effects of cultural, social, relational, and psychological variables on sexual function, well-being, and satisfaction.

9. The Management of Sexual Dysfunction:

- Progress made in applying a biopsychosocial framework to comprehend sexual dysfunctions (such as erectile dysfunction, low desire, and orgasmic disorders), taking into account contextual, relational, biological, and psychological aspects.

- Creation of individualized treatments, digital therapies, telehealth solutions, and integrative methods (such as medical treatments, sex therapy, psychotherapy, and mindfulness) to address sexual issues and enhance sexual function.

10. Consent, Technology, and Ethics:

- Data protection, informed permission, confidentiality, boundaries, and responsible use of digital technologies are among the ethical issues that should be taken into account while using technology in sexual psychology research, treatment, instruction, and interventions.

Investigating moral norms, best practices, and legal frameworks for using technology into sexual psychology practice while preserving moral principles and safeguarding the welfare and rights of clients.

These forthcoming developments in the field of sexual psychology are a reflection of multidisciplinary cooperation, continuing progress, changing cultural norms, and changing public perceptions of human sexuality. In order to address new issues, advance inclusion, promote fairness in sexual health, and advance knowledge in the field of sexual psychology, researchers, practitioners, educators, legislators, and activists will be essential players.

Developing Fields of Study in Sexual Psychology:

A wide range of subjects that are becoming more significant in understanding human sexuality, relationships, and well-being are included in emerging research fields in sexual psychology. These fields frequently show changing social views, advances in technology, changes in culture, and interdisciplinary teamwork. Several new fields of study in sexual psychology are as follows:

1 Digital Intimacy and Online Relationships: Studies on the effects of social media, virtual reality, dating apps, and digital platforms on sexual communication, intimacy, relationship dynamics, and sexual practices.
An investigation into how digital intimacy affects consent, privacy, emotional ties, sexual satisfaction, and the growth of intimacy skills in digital environments.

2. Well-being and Health of Sexual Minorities:
Examine variables such minority stress, identity formation, stigma, discrimination, and access to affirming healthcare. - Concentrate on the mental health, sexual well-being, and resilience of sexual minority communities, including LGBTQ+ people.
- Studies that examine how sexual orientation, gender identity, race, ethnicity, socioeconomic status, and other identities interact to influence the experiences and health consequences of sexual minorities.

3. Sexual Consent, Boundaries, and Communication: - Research looking at programs that promote consent education, sexual violence prevention, coercion, and affirmative consent behaviors as well as sexual boundaries and communication techniques.
- An examination of how people manage consent, handle sexual encounters, communicate their wishes, and set appropriate sexual boundaries in a range of partnerships and environments.

Studies pertaining to positive elements of sexuality, such as desire, arousal patterns, sexual satisfaction, and the significance of positive emotions, intimacy, and overall well-being in sexual experiences, are included in the fourth category.

Examining the elements that contribute to sexual enjoyment; variances in sexual response; individual variances in sexual preferences; and the influence of psychological elements (e.g., emotions, cognition) on the state of one's sexual life.

5. The Development of a Sexual Identity During Life:
- Longitudinal studies that look at how a person develops, explores, and affirms their sexual identity as they become older, taking into account influences from their personal, familial, societal, and cultural contexts.
Examining the fluidity, complexity, and alterations in labels, orientations, and sexual identities throughout time; this includes non-binary identities, sexual fluidity, and identity integration processes.

6. Technology-Aided Interventions and Therapies:
- Assessing the effectiveness of digital therapies, telehealth services, mobile applications, and technology-assisted interventions in treating sexual dysfunction, improving sexual well-being, and addressing relationship problems.
The creation of cutting-edge methods to promote sexual therapy, education, skill-building, and behavior change through the use of virtual reality, biofeedback, gamification, and online platforms.

7. Views from Around the World and Culture on Sexual Health:
- Cross-cultural research analyzing how migration, globalization, and cultural exchange impact sexual identities and behaviors; it also looks at cultural differences in sexual norms, beliefs, practices, attitudes, and experiences.
Research on the effects of cultural variables on sexual health outcomes and well-being; sexual health inequalities; access to sexual healthcare; and culturally competent treatments.

8. Perspectives on Sexual Health Throughout Life:
Research on age-related changes, sexual function, intimacy, and well-being, as well as sexual development in childhood, adolescence, adulthood, and older adults, is relevant to sexual health across the lifespan.
The investigation of sexual health requirements, encounters, and strategies for a range of age groups, such as senior citizens, those with impairments, and people managing life changes and medical issues.

Consent and Technology 9. Ethics: - Analysis of moral issues, legal frameworks, and optimal methods for integrating technology into sexual psychology research, counseling, teaching, and interventions while respecting the privacy, permission, confidentiality, and safety of clients.

- Studies that support sexual health and well-being through digital ethics, data security, informed consent procedures, boundary management, and responsible technology use.

Studies on sexual health disparities, access obstacles, and health equity issues among marginalized populations—such as sex workers, refugees, migrants, indigenous communities, people with disabilities, and socioeconomically disadvantaged groups—are included in the category of 10. Sexual Health in Marginalized Populations.

Examining the ways that intersectional factors—such as gender, race, ethnicity, sexual orientation, and socioeconomic status—affect sexual health outcomes, service accessibility, discrimination, and empowerment in marginalized communities.

These new topics of study in sexual psychology are a reflection of the field's dynamic nature, continuous discoveries, and the significance of tackling a range of issues related to human sexuality, relationships, and wellbeing. Innovative research and evidence-based approaches in sexual psychology can benefit individuals and communities by fostering sexual health equity, enhancing understanding, and improving quality of life for researchers, practitioners, educators, policymakers, and advocates.

Topics of Interest for Future Sexual Psychology Research:

Numerous subjects that are becoming more significant in understanding human sexuality, relationships, and well-being are included in the emerging fields of sexual psychology research. These fields frequently mirror changing culture, interdisciplinary cooperation, technology breakthroughs, and changing societal attitudes. In the field of sexual psychology, the following new areas are being studied:

Study on the effects of social media, virtual reality, dating apps, and digital platforms on intimacy, sexual communication, relationship dynamics, and sexual behaviors is the first step toward understanding digital intimacy and online relationships.
- Investigation of how digital intimacy affects consent, privacy, emotional ties, sexual satisfaction, and the growth of intimacy skills in digital environments.

2. Health and Welfare of Sexual Minorities:
- Pay attention to the resilience, mental health, and sexual health of sexual minority groups, such as LGBTQ+ people. Discuss issues including identity development, stigma, discrimination, and minority stress.
Research examines how the lives and health consequences of sexual minorities are shaped by the intersections of sexual orientation, gender identity, race, ethnicity, socioeconomic status, and other characteristics.

3. Studies on Affirmative Consent Practices, Sexual Boundaries, Communication Skills, and Consent Education Programs to Prevent Sexual Violence, Coercion, and Misconduct.
Investigation of how people in various relationships and situations manage consent, negotiate sex, express desires, and set appropriate sexual limits.

4. Research on Positive Sexuality and Sexual Pleasure: This area of study focuses on the positive aspects of sexuality, such as desire, arousal patterns, sexual

satisfaction, and the importance of pleasant emotions, intimacy, and overall wellbeing in sexual experiences.

- Research on the elements that contribute to sexual enjoyment, sexual response variances, individual variances in sexual preferences, and the influence of psychological elements (e.g., emotions, cognition) on any aspect of sexual health.

Section Five: Development of Sexual Identity Throughout Life:
- Studies that follow participants over time as they grow, explore, and affirm their sexual identities while taking into account societal, familial, cultural, and individual influences.
Investigation of the fluidity, complexities, and changes that occur in labels, orientations, and sexual identities throughout time; includes sexual fluidity, non-binary identities, and identity integration processes.

6. Therapies and interventions supported by technology:
- Assessment of mobile applications, digital therapies, telehealth services, and technology-assisted interventions for improving sexual well-being, treating relationship problems, sexual dysfunctions, and sexual health conditions.
Creation of novel strategies to enhance sexual therapy, education, skill-building, and behavior modification through the use of virtual reality, biofeedback, gamification, and online platforms.

7. Perceptions of Sexual Health in Culture and the World:
Cultural differences in sexual norms, attitudes, practices, beliefs, and experiences are the subject of cross-cultural research, which also looks at how migration, globalization, and cultural exchange affect sexual identities and behaviors.
Research on the effects of cultural factors on sexual health outcomes and well-being; accessibility to sexual healthcare; and studies on sexual health disparities; and culturally competent treatments.

8. Age- and life-span perspectives on sexual health:
Studies focusing on age-related changes, sexual function, intimacy, and well-being; these studies include sexual development in childhood, adolescence, adulthood, and older adults; these studies include sexual health across the lifespan.

Investigating the needs, experiences, and solutions related to sexual health for a range of age groups, such as senior citizens, people with disabilities, and people going through life changes and health issues.

9. Approval and Technology The ethical aspects of using technology in sexual psychology research, treatment, teaching, and interventions while respecting client privacy, permission, confidentiality, and safety are examined, along with legislative frameworks and best practices.
- Studies on the ethical and digital aspects of digital health and well-being; data security; informed consent procedures; boundary management; and responsible technology use.

10. Studies on Sexual Health in Marginalized Populations: These include studies on health equity issues, access barriers, and disparities in sexual health among marginalized populations such as sex workers, refugees, migrants, indigenous communities, people with disabilities, and socioeconomically disadvantaged groups.
Examining how intersectional factors—such as gender, race, ethnicity, sexual orientation, and socioeconomic status—affect underprivileged populations' empowerment, access to resources, experiences of discrimination, and results around sexual health.

The field's dynamic character, continuous knowledge gains, and the significance of addressing various facets of human sexuality, relationships, and well-being are all reflected in these novel study fields in sexual psychology. Innovative sexual psychology research and evidence-based methods can benefit individuals and communities by increasing sexual health equity, boosting understanding, and improving the quality of life for researchers, practitioners, educators, policymakers, and advocates.

The Promotion of Diversity and Inclusivity in Sexual Psychology:

A field that recognizes and honors the varied experiences, identities, and needs of people from different backgrounds must prioritize inclusivity and diversity in sexual psychology. To encourage diversity and inclusivity in sexual psychology, consider the following tactics and approaches:

1. Cultural Competence and Sensitivity: Gain knowledge of varied cultural beliefs, values, norms, and practices around sexuality by providing cultural competence training to mental health practitioners, researchers, educators, and policymakers.
In your work with clients or study on sexual psychology, stress the value of cultural sensitivity, respect for variety, and self-awareness.

The second viewpoint is the intersectionality perspective, which recognizes the intersections of many identities (such as gender, race, ethnicity, and sexual orientation) and how these intersections affect attitudes, experiences, and health outcomes related to sexual activity.
. Think about how different oppressions, privileges, and discrimination interact to influence how people perceive sexuality and have access to services for sexual health.

3. Inclusive vocabulary and Language: Steer clear of stigmatizing or pathologizing vocabulary in favor of inclusive language and terminology that represents a range of sexual identities, orientations, and manifestations.
. Encourage varied portrayals of sexual identities, bodies, relationships, and experiences in studies, teaching resources, the media, and professional associations.

4. Community Engagement and Collaboration: - Develop research initiatives, interventions, and policies that jointly address the particular needs and goals of underrepresented populations by collaborating with grassroots organizations, advocacy groups, and varied communities.

Assist in making sure that sexual psychology programs are inclusive, culturally appropriate, and sensitive to community opinions by working with activists, leaders, and cultural specialists.

Fifth, advancing equity and accessibility:
Promote readily available, reasonably priced sexual health services, mental health services, and educational materials that are inclusive of a range of demographics, such as those with disabilities, low language skills, or restricted access to healthcare.
Deal with structural obstacles to care, including differences in income, lack of culturally competent healthcare professionals, prejudice, and regional inequalities.

6. LGBTQ+ Affirming Care: - Offer LGBTQ+ affirming care that offers safe spaces for clients to explore their sexual identities and concerns while validating a range of sexual orientations, gender identities, and expressions.
In sexual psychology settings, include gender-affirming behaviors, affirmative therapy approaches, and LGBTQ+ inclusive policies.

7. Techniques Based on Trauma:
To address the effects of trauma, violence, and discrimination on people's sexual health, relationships, and well-being, adopt trauma-informed approaches in sexual psychology practice, research, and education.
Offer resources, consent-focused interventions, and trauma-sensitive care to victims of sexual assault or trauma.

8. Empowerment and Advocacy: - Encourage projects that advance social justice, human rights, and sexual health equity for all people, irrespective of their identities or backgrounds. - Provide marginalized communities with the tools they need to advocate for their rights to sexual health, access to services, and representation in sexual psychology research, education, and policy-making.

9. Training and Education Programs: - Provide sexual psychology practitioners with training programs, workshops, and opportunities for continuing education to improve their proficiency in working with various groups, as well as their awareness of cultural competency and diversity.

- Include diversity and inclusivity as a core component of clinical training, professional development activities, and sexual psychology curriculums.

In order to inform evidence-based interventions, policy reforms, and advocacy initiatives, research on disparities, inequities, and impediments to sexual health and well-being among underrepresented populations should be conducted.
Encourage the implementation of laws and programs that support public health efforts, research funding, and the practice of sexual psychology with a focus on equity, diversity, and cultural competence.

These tactics can be used to address the various sexual needs, experiences, and identities of people and groups all over the world in a way that is more affirming, helpful, and successful by fostering an inclusive and varied culture in the field of sexual psychology.

Advancing Sexual Research: Ethical Considerations:

In order to protect the rights, privacy, dignity, and well-being of participants, researchers, and the larger community, ethical considerations are crucial to the advancement of sexual research. Sexual research should be guided by the following important ethical considerations:

1. Obtain voluntary, ongoing, and informed consent from subjects participating in sexual research by outlining the study's goals, methods, possible risks and benefits, confidentiality precautions, and subjects' right to discontinue participation at any moment without facing consequences.
Assure participants are able to give informed permission, supply information in understandable and suitable languages and forms, and respond to inquiries and concerns raised prior to, during, and following the research project.

2. Confidentiality and Privacy: - Reduce the likelihood of data breaches, unauthorized access, or inadvertent disclosures that could endanger participants' safety, reputation, or well-being. - Provide participants with limited access to sensitive information, secure storage, de-identification methods, and data encryption.

3. Autonomy and Agency Respect: - Give participants the freedom to make decisions about their identities, habits, and sexual health as well as their participation in study.
Steer clear of pressure, undue influence, or coercion as they could impair participants' capacity to make free-will decisions about participating in sexual research.

4. Avoiding Harm and Minimizing hazards: - Evaluate and reduce any possible hazards—physical, psychological, social, or emotional—that may arise from sexual research. These risks include those related to stigma, prejudice, discomfort, discomfort, or unforeseen outcomes.
- Offer participants who might suffer negative effects or need extra help during or after the research the proper support, referrals, debriefing, and follow-up care.

5. Touchy Subjects and Vulnerable Groups: - Treat touchy subjects pertaining to sexuality, sex practices, gender identity, sexual orientation, or sexual trauma with tact, understanding, and cultural competency.
- When doing research on vulnerable groups, such as children, people with cognitive disabilities, victims of sexual assault, or marginalized communities, get additional ethical clearances, informed consent procedures, and protections.

6. Steer clear of Exploitation and Objectification: Steer clear of taking advantage of subjects or objectifying people in sexual study because of their identities, experiences, or sexual traits.
Avoid sensationalism, stigmatization, and stereotypes; instead, use polite language, imagery, and representations that support participants' humanity, diversity, and dignity.

7. Cultural Sensitivity and Inclusivity: - Take into account sexuality-related cultural norms, attitudes, beliefs, and behaviors when doing research with varied populations or in culturally diverse environments.
Involve stakeholders, community members, and cultural advisers to make sure that research questions, techniques, interpretations, and recommendations are courteous, pertinent, and culturally sensitive.

8. Accountability and Transparency in Reporting: - Clearly state in publications, speeches, and public communications the study methodology, results, constraints, sources of funding, and ethical issues.
To maintain accountability, integrity, and transparency, abide by professional codes of ethics, institutional review board (IRB) rules, ethical norms in sexual research, and legal obligations.

9. Beneficence and Social Responsibility: - Put participants' rights, welfare, and safety first. Give beneficence (doing good) and non-maleficence (prevent harm) top priority in the planning, execution, and dissemination of research.
Examine the possible effects of sexual research on society, taking into account how policies, practices, lobbying, education, and public health interventions may be affected in order to encourage social responsibility and beneficial outcomes.

10. Ongoing Ethical contemplation and Oversight: To address new ethical issues, conundrums, and best practices in sexual research, practitioners, ethics committees, and researchers should engage in continuing ethical contemplation, discussion, and training.
Provide strong ethical supervision procedures, accountability frameworks, and monitoring systems to guarantee that ethical norms, guidelines, and principles are followed at every stage of the study process.

Researchers can advance knowledge, promote participant well-being, contribute to evidence-based interventions, and uphold ethical integrity in the field of sexual psychology by giving priority to these ethical considerations and incorporating ethical frameworks, guidelines, and best practices into sexual research.

CHAPTER THIRTEEN

In Conclusion:

In order to develop holistic strategies that support fulfilling sexual experiences, healthy relationships, and general well-being, synthesizing information for sexual well-being entails combining ideas from diverse disciplines, study areas, and perspectives. The following is a summary of important elements and methods for improving sexual well-being:

1. Biopsychosocial Approach: - Acknowledge how social, psychological, and biological elements interact to shape sexual well-being. Think about the ways that relationships, cultural settings, societal norms, cognitive processes, emotions, anatomy, physiology, hormones, and genetics affect sexual health and enjoyment.

2. Sexual Health Literacy: - Encourage sexual health literacy by disseminating accurate, fact-based knowledge about anatomy, sexual development, reproductive health, STIs, consent, pleasure, communication skills, diversity in sexual orientation, and rights.
- Give people the tools they need to make educated decisions, negotiate sexual situations, get the care they need, and adopt healthy habits that enhance their sexual wellbeing.

3. Positive Sexuality and Pleasure: Stress the significance of erotic well-being, positive sexuality, and sexual pleasure as vital elements of general health and life satisfaction.
In consensual and courteous relationships, promote introspection, self-discovery, and dialogue about fantasies, desires, preferences, boundaries, and consent.

4. Relationship Quality and Intimacy: - Emphasize how wholesome partnerships, emotional closeness, communication, empathy, and mutual respect all contribute to the development of healthy sexual behavior.
* Help people and couples improve their emotional connection, learn how to be intimate, resolve conflict, and have fulfilling sex.

5. Inclusive and Affirming Practices: - Promote diversity, inclusivity, and cultural sensitivity in public health campaigns, healthcare services, counseling, and education on sexual health.
- Address the stigma, prejudice, and obstacles to care that marginalized groups—such as members of the LGBTQ+ community, racial and ethnic minorities, those with disabilities, and socioeconomically disadvantaged groups—face.

6. Trauma-Informed Care: - Use trauma-informed strategies to address coercion, violence, sexual trauma, and abuse while offering survivors empathetic and empowered assistance.
- In sexual health interventions, therapy, and advocacy activities, give safety, autonomy, consent, and trauma sensitivity first priority.

7. Consent Culture and Respectful Communication: - Encourage the development of a culture in which sexual encounters are conducted with affirmative consent, deference, and ethical communication. This culture should emphasize limits, mutual understanding, open communication, and attentive listening.
Promote community norms that value consent, respect individual autonomy, and forbid sexual misbehavior or injury. These include bystander intervention training and consent education.

8. Comprehensive Sexual Education: - Promote comprehensive programs that educate people about sexuality that cover a range of topics, including gender identities, relationships, pleasure, consent, contraception, STIs, reproductive rights, and social justice.
Encourage age-appropriate, scientifically validated sexual education at healthcare facilities, educational institutions, and online to equip people with the information, abilities, and attitudes needed to make healthy sexual decisions.

9. Accessible and Inclusive healthcare: - Guarantee that people, irrespective of their identities, experiences, or origins, have access to inclusive, affirming, and nonjudgmental sexual healthcare services that address their various needs.

- Encourage sexual healthcare providers to treat patients with cultural competency, LGBTQ+ affirming care, trauma-informed practices, and collaborative approaches to sexual health issues.

10. Research, Advocacy, and Policy Change: Encourage studies that contribute to our knowledge of sexual health inequities, effective interventions, and evidence-based practices in public health, sexual psychology, and policy.
- Push for systemic reforms, financing, and policy adjustments that advance social justice, health equity, inclusion, and sexual rights for all people.

We may establish supportive environments, give people agency, cultivate healthy relationships, and encourage good attitudes and behaviors that support holistic sexual health and flourishing by combining information and putting multifaceted approaches to sexual well-being into practice.

The Significance of Continued Research and Education:

In the subject of sexual psychology, there are a number of reasons why it is important to have ongoing research and education.

1. Increasing Knowledge: Research contributes to our growing understanding of human sexuality, including relationships, growth, behaviors, experiences, and well-being. Developments in sexual psychology and related fields are possible because it enables us to investigate novel ideas, theories, and factual data.

2. Improving Interventions: The results of research are used to guide the creation of evidence-based therapies, methods, and interventions to address mental health disorders, trauma, sexual dysfunction, and questions about sexual health. More research is needed to improve results, hone interventions, and customize strategies for each person.

3. Promoting Sexual Health: Education is essential for empowering people, communities, healthcare professionals, educators, legislators, and other stakeholders around sexual health literacy and awareness. Programs, courses, and materials offering comprehensive sexual education can promote safer behaviors, positive attitudes toward sexuality, and informed decision-making.

Educating people about sexuality, sexual identities, orientations, and behaviors can help dispel myths, prejudices, and stigma associated with it. Education creates an environment that is more accepting and supportive of a range of sexual orientations and experiences by advancing truthful information, inclusivity, and respect for variety.

5. Preventing Sexual Violence and Harm: Research and education initiatives support treatments, awareness campaigns, and prevention tactics meant to lessen coercion, harassment, abuse, and exploitation in the context of sexual violence. In

order to encourage a culture of consent and prevent harm, education about healthy relationships, limits, and consent is crucial.

6. Fostering LGBTQ+ Communities: The promotion of LGBTQ+ affirming care, inclusive practices, cultural competence, and advocacy for LGBTQ+ rights and well-being are all made possible by ongoing research and educational programs. Having more knowledge about sexual health issues can help LGBTQ+ populations access resources and support more easily and with less stigma, prejudice, and inequality.

7. Improving Professional Training: Continual education and training programs guarantee that mental health professionals, educators, therapists, counselors, and healthcare providers remain up to date on ethical guidelines, best practices, and cultural competence when it comes to serving diverse populations and handling delicate sexual issues.

Research outcomes and educational endeavors serve as a valuable source of information for evidence-based policy formulation, advocacy campaigns, and public health initiatives that center around sexual rights, health equity, consent education, reproductive justice, LGBTQ+ rights, and social determinants of sexual health.

9. Enhancing Quality of Life and Well-Being: Full well-being, wholesome relationships, emotional closeness, resilience, and self-worth are the goals of ongoing sexual psychology research and educational programs. Having a meaningful and genuine sexual life is made possible by education on self-care, body acceptance, healthy sexuality, and communication techniques.

To sum up, to advance the fields of sexual psychology and related fields—and to improve professional training, inform policy, support LGBTQ+ communities, address stigma, promote sexual health, prevent harm, and advance knowledge—more research and education are needed. By doing this, we can help people navigate their sexual experiences, relationships, and identities with dignity, autonomy, and respect by fostering an environment that is more educated, inclusive, and supportive.

Empowering People for Healthy and Fulfilling Sexual Lives:

Giving people the information, abilities, tools, and support they need to make wise choices, handle sensual situations, form wholesome bonds with others, and put their sexual health first is a key component of empowering them for healthy and fulfilling sexual lives. In this framework, the following are important tactics for empowering individuals:

Providing Comprehensive Sexual Education: Provide comprehensive programs covering a variety of subjects, such as anatomy, physiology, sexual diversity, relationships, communication skills, STIs, reproductive health, consent, enjoyment, and sexual diversity. At schools, communities, healthcare facilities, and online, disseminate evidence-based, age-appropriate information.

2. Fostering Self-Confidence and Body Positivity: Foster self-acceptance, body positivity, and self-esteem by promoting a positive body image, challenging unattainable beauty standards, and celebrating a variety of bodies, shapes, sizes, and abilities. Encourage self-care and self-confidence by offering training, tools, and campaigns.

3. Creating an Environment of Open Communication: Promote courteous, sincere, and candid dialogue regarding sexual preferences, expectations, boundaries, and desires. Assist in communicating wants and concerns about sexuality with assertiveness, empathy, active listening, and effective communication techniques.

The fourth strategy is to cultivate a culture of consent that values ethical communication, respect for personal space, and affirmative consent. Inform people that getting explicit, passionate, and continuous consent is crucial before having any kind of sexual activity. Supplies, seminars, and instruction on consent education, bystander intervention, and identifying abuse or coercive indicators should be made available.

Fifth, Handling Discrimination and Stigma: Dispel falsehoods, prejudice, stigma, and discrimination around sexuality, gender identities, sexual orientations, and a variety of sexual behaviors. Embrace diversity, uphold individual autonomy, and encourage people to express who they truly are without fear of prejudice or condemnation by creating inclusive and nurturing environments.

6. Trauma-Informed Assistance:. Those who have suffered from sexual trauma, abuse, coercion, or violence should receive care and assistance that is trauma-informed. Provide survivors' safety, empowerment, autonomy, and recovery with a focus on resources, therapy, and nonjudgmental, confidential services.

7. Access to Sexual Health Services: Take steps to guarantee that everyone has equal access to inclusive, accepting, and reasonably priced sexual health services. These services include mental health support, contraception, STI testing and treatment, reproductive healthcare, and sexual counseling. Take action against obstacles that prevent people from receiving care, including financial limitations, ignorance, stigma, and restricted access to healthcare for underserved groups.

8. Empowering LGBTQ+ Communities: Support members of the LGBTQ+ community by advocating for LGBTQ+ affirming treatment, cultural sensitivity, and inclusive practices in the fields of education, healthcare, and community services. Fight for the rights, visibility, representation, and resources that LGBTQ+ people require and face in relation to their particular sexual health concerns.

9. Encouraging Safer Sexual Practices: Promote safer sexual practices, risk reduction tactics, and harm reduction methods to people in order to stop STIs, unwanted pregnancies, and issues related to sexual health. Inform them about the use of condoms, available forms of contraception, the need for routine STI testing, and immunization against HPV and other STDs.

Building Well-Being and Resilience 10 Help people deal with obstacles, pressures, and emotional problems pertaining to sexuality, relationships, and identity by providing mental health assistance, coping mechanisms, and resilience-building programs. To address issues related to sexual health and enhance general quality of life, encourage holistic well-being, self-care routines, mindfulness, and constructive coping techniques.

Communities and individuals can benefit from healthier, more fulfilling sexual lives if these strategies are put into practice and supportive environments are established that enable people to make educated decisions, communicate effectively, access resources, and advocate for their sexual rights and well-being.

www.ingramcontent.com/pod-product-compliance
Lightning Source LLC
Chambersburg PA
CBHW081546250726
48653CB00009B/3289